Golf at the North Pole:
The Artic and the Ancient Game

– A G D. MARAN –

An environmentally friendly book printed and bound in England by
www.printondemand-worldwide.com

Mixed Sources
Product group from well-managed forests, and other controlled sources
www.fsc.org Cert no. TT-COC-002641
© 1996 Forest Stewardship Council

PEFC Certified
This product is from sustainably managed forests and controlled sources
www.pefc.org

This book is made entirely of chain-of-custody materials

FastPrint Publishing

www.fast-print.net/store.php

Golf at the North Pole: The Arctic
and the Ancient Game
Copyright © A G D Maran 2013

All rights reserved

No part of this book may be reproduced in any form by photocopying
or any electronic or mechanical means, including information storage
or retrieval systems, without permission in writing from both the
copyright owner and the publisher of the book.

The right of A G D Maran to be identified as the author of this work has
been asserted by him in accordance with the Copyright, Designs and
Patents Act 1988 and any subsequent amendments thereto.

A catalogue record for this book is available from the British Library

ISBN 978-178035-704-1

First published 2013 by
FASTPRINT PUBLISHING
Peterborough, England.

Contents

Chapter 1   4
Meeting an Astronaut

Chapter 2   13
The North Poles

Chapter 3   22
Getting Ready

Chapter 4   35
Meeting Mohammed

Chapter 5   45
Passengers and crew

Chapter 6   59
Sea sickness

Chapter 7   66
Eskimos and Myths

Chapter 8   77
The Arctic; geography and ownership

Chapter 9 The Barrow Boys	87
Chapter 10 Early American explorers	96
Chapter 11 Wild Life	103
Chapter 12 Does anyone know we're here?	110
Chapter 13 Norwegian of the Millenium	118
Chapter 14 Foreign Golf	135
Chapter 15 More Foreign Golf	146
Chapter 16 Hot air balloons	158
Chapter 17 The Royal explorer	175
Chapter 18 The Red Tent	189
Chapter 19 Cheating	204
Chapter 20 The Peary Cook story	213
Chapter 21 The Aftermath	236

Chapter 22　　　　　　　　　　　　　　　　**247**
Arriving at the Pole

Chapter 23　　　　　　　　　　　　　　　　**256**
Setting up the Tournament

Chapter 24　　　　　　　　　　　　　　　　**266**
The Tournament

Chapter 25　　　　　　　　　　　　　　　　**277**
Coming Home

Chapter One
Meeting An Astronaut

The idea of playing golf at the North Pole came to me after I'd had a conversation with Neil Armstrong, the first man to step onto the surface of the Moon. I met him in the Big Room of the Royal and Ancient Golf Club of St Andrews just two years before he died.

The Big Room is just that -- a very big room about 20 yards long, lit by three enormous crystal chandeliers and containing many low soft leather armchairs, a large table in the window bay and several other smaller round tables at which four golfers can enjoy their nineteenth hole refreshment; exactly as you would imagine appropriate for any gentleman's club (sorry, no lady members yet).

What is different from any other gentleman's club is the fact that around the walls are old fashioned wooden golf lockers of hardly any depth and apparently useless for today's golf armoury, but brass name-plates declare who the present owners are. Outweighing the kudos that might come from having one's name on a locker in the

Golf at the North Pole

Big Room is the fact that after having waited about 45 years for the privilege, your life expectancy will now be of the order of just over 5 years -- if averages are to be believed.

On the walls above the lockers are large portraits of the Queen, Earl Haig, the Duke of Windsor, Tom Morris and many other famous past Captains including Edward, Duke of York looking like the 1930s poster boy that he was.

There are two large fireplaces on each side wall and in winter months both fires burn all day guarded by magnificent iron and leather 'bum-warmers' on which golfers might sit until their temperatures have recovered to normal after braving the fierce south-westerlies of the Links.

The Big Room was the central part of a building constructed by the members of the St Andrews Society of Golfers in 1854 and is certainly the most recognised and most illustrated golfing establishment in the world. In the eighteenth century while many young English aristocrats might go on the Grand Tour of Europe to improve their knowledge of Art and Culture there was not a corresponding number of aesthetic Scottish noblemen following in their footsteps. The Scots usually had more interest in the basic life skills of eating, drinking and wagering, all usually centred around their main activity which would be playing golf on the St Andrews Links. These were not men who enjoyed the aesthetic pleasures of beauty, art and literature and there were probably two reasons that kept them at home-- the lack of travel facilities to Europe and an intense satisfaction with life on their estates and in their clubs.

The Room they built has an enormous bay window looking out over the first tee of the most famous golf course in the world, the Old Course, where, almost every hour of every day one can see golfers of various nationalities tee off.

One sees fewer and fewer local golfers there because they find it increasingly difficult to get starting times because of the worldwide demand but they can instantly be recognised by their familiarity with their surroundings, the lack of appreciation of the aura of that famous first tee, their invariable long straight drives and the speed with which they move off the tee and walk briskly down the fairway.

They are very different from the visitors - usually American, European or Japanese - for whom this is their 'Big Day'. It is the day they have looked forward to most of their golfing lives and they and their friends will have spent a lot of money getting here and getting a time and so they are going to enjoy it and record it. Those who were not lucky enough to get a time for themselves will start queueing up at the starter's box around 3am in the hope that some time during the next 15 hours someone might not turn up.

Often we sit in the Big Room and watch four golfers, four caddies and often four to six friends who will accompany the game with cameras. They move with ethereal sublimeness from the tee towards the Swilcan Burn where at least one of them will have deposited their approach shot to the green. Will they be bothered? Not a bit of it. The more hazards the better -- it's all part of their St Andrews experience.

During the winter there would only be a few local members sitting around in the Big Room, but twice a year-- for a week in May and three weeks in September-- the good and great of golf arrive from all over the world, congregate for golf competitions and enjoy fellowship, dining and drinking but, these days, very little wagering.

Who are these fortunate members who for a relatively small subscription get access to all 7 courses in St Andrews? You certainly do not 'apply' to join; well you might, but all you'd get back would be a polite letter from the Members' Secretary informing you of the normal procedure, which is that you wait for an invitation. Even after a friend has invited you to become a member, the dominoes must fall in your direction. You yourself must be at least a competent golfer if not a rather good one; you must have done something to help the game of golf, even such a lowly task as volunteering to help in something like an obscure Boys' Open where you might help sweep the water off the greens. Most people however have done something more, for example been Captain of their club, sat on some golf committees or played representative golf.

But that's only a third of the problem. Anyone who invites you to be put up for membership must have been a member for at least five years, he must not be involved currently in either proposing or seconding anyone else and he must write a convincing recommendation as to why you would make a suitable member. He has to find two other members who are currently uninvolved in helping someone else along the rocky path to membership and they too must convince the Membership Committee that they not only know you well but know why you would be a good member if accepted.

The final third lies in the hands of the Membership Committee whose criteria are seldom spoken of and whose rejection of an application might put the proposer in the position of the long lists of "The Man Who ..." cartoons made famous by the cartoonist, H E Bateman, in the inter-war years. If they accept the nomination then the nominee's name is entered into the 'Book', a large ledger-like volume which lies on the table in the Big Room in the club. The 'Book' contains all the names of those who are waiting for membership and gives an indication of the support they are receiving; this comes in the form of letters of support.

The two thousand members of the club are apprised of your nomination and they are invited to write letters of support provided they know you personally; the names of supporters are entered into the 'Book' and when enough have been received the person becomes eligible for membership--- but then has to wait for a vacancy. This whole process can take 5 - 7 years. But once in, you are in the greatest golf club in the world.

At the small club shop you will likely purchase a club tie, probably a pullover and a few logoed shirts and (only if you don't understand these things) club buttons for your blazer.

Although the Club doesn't own a course it does make and interpret the Rules along with the USGA, decides what equipment is legal and what is not and as well as the British Open Championship and British Amateur, the Club runs many other more minor tournaments. They do this with a relatively small permanent staff who are helped by dozens of members who give freely of their time (sometimes more than 6 weeks a year) to make sure that all this is possible. Because of all these activities members have to be potential 'givers' and certainly not 'takers'.

If you're any good you may be invited to sit on some of the committees possibly starting with the Rules Committee, or if you have a scientific bent, the Equipment Committee. From there you may progress to the exalted heights of the Membership, the Championship or the Business Committee. And at the zenith of your golf career you may achieve a place on the General Committee.

This is not the route that I followed almost 40 years ago.

I was a surgeon; measuring my skill level would be difficult but suffice it to say that I did surgery very much better than I played golf. An important Member came to see me with a tumour. The operation went well and on his last visit he growled at me in an aristocratic gravelly voice "You a Member of the Club, my boy?"-- I was younger then. "No" I stammered, really not quite sure what he was talking about. "I'll see to it" he said, and that was the last I heard from him until a letter dropped through my door a few years later telling me that I had been accepted as a Member.

Unfortunately, since I was a rubbish golfer, perhaps the worst in the club and certainly regarded by my friends as the easiest half crown (pre-decimalisation) on the links, membership went to my head. For some time my behaviour could only be regarded as outrageous. Whenever I rested my golf bag on a rack, rail or wall I'd make sure that the bag tag saying 'Member of the R&A' was facing outwards so that every one knew that I was a VIP golfer -- who was just about to have an 'off-day'. I wore the club regalia at all times and for a time my golf even improved because I set about practising. I learned the Rules, studied the Decisions of the Rules Committee and became a 'Rules bore'.

Such behaviour however came to an end one day on the Old Course when I felt I was being held up by a group of four players with caddies. I went up to one of the caddies and told him he should know better than to hold up members of the R&A. The reply somehow lacked the respect I thought that I and my fellow members were due. He looked me in the eye and said "The R&A are a lot of f...ing wankers!" That seemed to carry a certain finality and it managed to bring a well-needed reappraisal of my position.

Over the years my golf has steadily deteriorated from the 'bad' through the 'awful' to the 'unspeakable'. I eventually realised that I would never be any good at it but I still treasured my membership and it was only this fact that stopped me giving up the game. If I couldn't play golf, could I administer it? The short answer is 'No'. I did however volunteer for the 'coolie' type of jobs such as marshalling at tournaments or holding up 'Quiet Please" boards but I realised that holding up a board on the final hole of the Open was going to be the summit of my golfing achievements.

So, faced with a lifetime certainty of playing dreadful golf, could I achieve anything of merit from all my efforts? Certainly I could be of no use to the Club other than eating, drinking and paying a subscription, but as I was able to travel the world in my professional capacity-- I found that everywhere I went the golfing red carpet was laid out for that most exalted of men, a member of the R&A!

I decided that my golfing odyssey would not be to lower my handicap to single figures, to join lots of other clubs or to attempt to win prizes. What I would do would be to try and play as many courses in as many countries as I could.

For about 30 years that was the path I followed. I started with the Home Countries and by dint of playing lots of little unknown courses I soon built up an impressive number. As I travelled on my professional duties I often took my clubs along and while others might make a list of buildings, galleries and natural wonders to visit, I had a list of accessible golf courses. My golf library had many similar volumes listing 'Famous Golf Courses of the World' and before travelling I would study and try to memorise the holes so as to extract maximum enjoyment from the forthcoming experiences.

But let's get back to Neil Armstrong that afternoon in the Big Room. By the time I met him, I was getting bored with 'collecting' courses and countries and I was no longer travelling so much. I asked Neil, a very competent golfer, why Alan Shepard rather than himself had hit a golf ball on the Moon. I knew this because when the commander of the second Apollo to land on the Moon was put forward for membership of the Club his proposal carried the laconic comment "Hit first 6 iron on surface of Moon".

Neil said that there were more basic worries and challenges awaiting him as the first man to "That's one small step for man, and one giant leap for mankind".

He ignored my response: "Such as falling through the crust?"

But talking about golf on the Moon widened my horizons. I would no longer do this meaningless 'counting exercise' of playing in lots of different places. I was approaching my ninth decade and I needed something quite different to cap the collection. Obviously it had to be on this planet - I was too old and too poor to get a space flight - and it had to be somewhere that I could get to with reasonable ease.

And after a bit of thought, I decided that that place would be the North Pole.

Chapter 2
The North Pole(S)

Why did I immediately think of the North rather than the South Pole?

After all, to a Brit, the North Pole is sort of 'foreign'. Little-known Americans such as Robert Byrd, Robert Peary and Frederick Cook had hogged all the headlines until our own Wally Herbert walked right across the top of the world in 1968.

It was the South Pole that was British. After all hadn't we been trying to reach it since 1901? My boyhood hero Captain Robert Falcon Scott led the Discovery Expedition in that year, and perished in a polar attempt a decade later in a valiant endeavour to beat that 'awful foreigner' Amundsen.

Scott was the stuff of dreams, a hero whom little boys in the 1930s and '40s were brought up to admire. Even that wonderfully unusual second name, Falcon, was designed surely to describe a man of superhuman qualities. But not only was he beaten to the Pole, his spirit was so broken, that he and his colleagues perished on the return journey.

At least that was what they told me at school.

So why not follow Scott and play a golf hole at the South Pole in his honour.

Two reasons-- it costs too much and it's doubtful if permission would be granted to construct a hole and hold a tournament there.

Although lots of cruise ships go to Antarctica, they only land on the periphery of the huge continent a very long way from the South Pole.

After a lot of research, the least expensive way I discovered of getting to the South Pole (other than being an invited scientist) was to get myself to McMurdo Sound (in itself expensive) and then get on an American plane which would fly me there and back in a day for not far short of $50,000.

As well as the expense there is the fact that the people on the Amundsen-Scott station, the permanent South Pole station for scientific research, do not want tourists contaminating their scientific work and, although I never asked, I presumed that knocking golf balls around, given the propensity of non-experts to hit it sideways, might present a risk of damage to millions of dollars' worth of equipment.

On the other hand I found it difficult to imagine that with hundreds of American scientists passing through the Amundsen-Scott station (which is possibly not as comfortable as a Hyatt Regency but certainly a big step up from a Travelodge) it would be inconceivable to believe that not a single one of them has ever in the past been granted permission to hit a golf ball (provided they retrieved it) so that he could bring a photo back to his Country Club.

Golf at the North Pole

Certainly the South Pole shows much more potential for planning a golf course than the North Pole because after you get over the Beaumont Glacier it's flat, flat, flat. Even I could lay out an attractive nine, if not eighteen holes on the site of the Amundsen-Scott station.

Early in 2012 a group of British adventurers led by former SAS officer Neil Laughton played a cricket match at the South Pole to commemorate Captain Scott's arrival in 1912. They played against an 'international' team of scientists stationed at the Amundsen-Scott base and, although the temperature was minus 35 degrees, the Brits won. Considering that none of the opposition had probably ever seen, never mind played cricket before, this win was not at all that surprising.

I have tried to research whether or not any of Scott's crew took a golf club on that last tragic journey. The only likely golfer would have been the Scotsman, Henry Bowes from Greenock, who died with Scott. There is however no record of this and since Henry was a lieutenant in the Royal Navy it is rather unlikely that he had membership of any golf club. Perhaps, since most of the exploration party were associated in one way or another with the Navy, not the most golf-minded of the Services, it is not surprising that a bag of clubs was not in the manifest of the *Terra Nova*, Scott's 1911 ship.

By chance, as I was thinking about my proposed trip, I received in my mail a brochure from a firm called Arcturus, based in the unlikely spot of Devon. This offered passages to the North Pole (with a barbecue on the ice on arrival--- whoopee!) and it seemed the right price at the right time. I had always associated the Polar explorations, and especially Arctic trips, with bearded hard men from the Shetlands, Iceland or northern Canada. But the agent was neither bearded nor male; she was Fiona Brijnath.

I signed up for the trip but soon had second thoughts when Fiona expressed doubts both as to the possibility of my being allowed golf clubs aboard the boat and even if that was allowed, she doubted if I would be allowed to play since golf it might pollute a preservation area. She reminded me that even relics of past expeditions had to be left untouched in the Arctic and so she very much doubted that hitting golf balls would be considered 'green' in an environment that was so carefully protected.

As a long time member of the R&A, I took a bit of exception to the latter suggestion and explained that, while my golf might be interspersed with the occasional shank, it was non- toxic to anyone except myself or possibly hypersensitive playing partners. I put her interpretation of this greenest of green sports down to the fact that there are few decent courses where she lives. At least she did not promulgate the usual reason for not doing something -- Health and Safety -- and so I generously took the view that, as a non-golfer who had clearly spent much of her life communing with Nature, she obviously had no idea what she was talking about. Sympathetic as I was to her misspent youth, there followed an angry exchange of emails balancing carrying golf clubs against money back. I won this well-fought battle at the eighteenth and so planning went forwards.

With the decision made and my bank account decidedly slimmed down, I decided to work out the fine

Golf at the North Pole

detail of the trip ahead. The transporting vehicle was going to be a Russian nuclear-powered ice-breaker called *50 Years of Victory*. Russia has six such vessels and they are normally used throughout the winter to lead convoys along the northern coast of Russia. The reason why Russia has to keep ice-breakers in service is because there are parts of Siberia where there is no adequate road system and occasionally equipment has to be moved that is too large for air transport. In the winter, sailing along the north coast of Russia is generally possible apart from three what are called 'choke-points'. These are places where thick ice forms between off-shore islands and the coast to a depth that makes sea travel impossible. From west to east the three sets of islands are Novaya Zemlya, Severnaya Zemlya and, furthest east, the New Siberian Islands. But in the summer, when the ice has gone, the ice-breakers are no longer needed and since the nineteen nineties, they have been rented to American companies so that they can make money from taking tourists to the North Pole. They will take people not to any old North Pole but to the True and real North Pole.

Why do I say 'any old North Pole'? That's because there are three other North Poles -- the magnetic, the geomagnetic and the inaccessible poles.

The magnetic pole was discovered by one of the early Royal Navy explorers -- one of the many sent out by Sir John Barrow -- the so-called 'Barrow Boys'.

John Ross was trapped on Baffin Island for 4 years in the 1830s and so he had plenty of time to figure out why his compass was behaving erratically near the 70th parallel. Facing the difficulties that he did, he might well have been forgiven for thinking that he was losing his marbles, but he remained rational enough to work out that he was at a point where the Earth's magnetic field pointed directly downwards. This was due to the fact that the Earth's axis is not a vertical line but is a line or axis that is 23 degrees to the vertical and that the Magnetic Pole is affected by the circulation of molten iron within the hot and liquid outer core of the Earth. This point is therefore constantly moving but is always well south of the True Pole.

About 5 degrees north of this is the geomagnetic pole which is where the geomagnetic field that surrounds the earth goes vertically upwards into space as the magnetosphere; this is the best spot from which to see the Auroral lights but it doesn't count as being an alternative North Pole.

And finally there is the pole of Inaccessibility; this is the furthest point from land in the Arctic Ocean and is really of interest only to the type of explorer who either wanders the Arctic or who is walking across the top of the world like the late Sir Wally Herbert.

The True North Pole, which is where I was aiming to go, is where all the lines of longitude converge and so there is no true time at the North Pole. You can set your watch to whatever time you want but if you advance or retreat 15 degrees you'll have to adjust your time an hour forward or back depending on which direction you decided to move. I've never managed to confirm the possibility that if you walked anticlockwise round a point as indicated on your GPS as 90 degrees north 365 times you could claim that you could be a year younger by the number of times you crossed the date-line. I have a feeling however that that is monstrously incorrect or else someone would have marketed the opportunity.

Both the South and the North Poles move all the time due to the perturbation in the rotation of the earth, but the South Pole moves very much less than the North. At the South Pole, which is on the land mass of Antarctica, the movement is only about ten metres a year and its new position is ceremonially adjusted each New Year's Day at the Amundsen-Scott Station, which sits on 9000 feet of ice fixed to the underlying land mass.

The North Pole, on the other hand, sits not on land but on sea, the Arctic Ocean, and thus moves much more because the normal earthly perturbation is amplified by the drift of the ice mass on the sea.

Over the centuries, the ice has become thinner and so the drift has increased because there is less ice to move. Picture an upside down cracked saucer sitting in a huge bowl of fluid where the fluid is 'swirling. The saucer would move and the 'cracks' might open and the pieces of the saucer would change position.

In 2005, Tom Avery took a team to the North Pole using similar equipment to early explorers but with the added advantage of GPS which tells you exactly where you are at any time. With this technology he was able to be certain that he was at the Pole; but after camping for a night at 90 degrees north, he found they had drifted half a kilometre from the point at which they had declared themselves to be 'at the North Pole'.

The Arctic Ocean is always in motion due to a current known as the North Atlantic Gyre, which is the source of the Gulf Stream. The Gyre is driven by Trade Winds and the forces of the turning earth and sweeps first from West Africa to the Caribbean and then along the coast of North America. When it reaches the New England coast, it curves east and crosses the Grand Banks south of Newfoundland, where it melts any icebergs drifting south from Greenland as if they were ice cubes in a cup of Starbuck's coffee. The Drift then moves northeastwards between Scotland and Iceland, making a small zone of Scotland so warm that palm trees grow on the west coast . This is at a place called Poolewe, which lies between 57 and 58 degrees north, which is the same latitude as northern Labrador.

By the time the Gyre reaches the north of Norway, the still warm and salty tropical water collides with the southward drifting ice of the polar pack in the vicinity of the Spitsbergen archipelago. As it cools, the salty tropical water becomes denser than the cold Arctic water and so it sinks and turns southward to flow deep in the ocean, eventually to replace the water sent north by the surface currents of the original Gyre.

The chaos in the water flow and the big difference in temperatures as different currents meet, create a veritable treasure trove of nutrients in the food chain. As the ice pack melts it gives off its concentrated bloom of early summer algae and so plankton flourishes, creating a copious larder for fish; shrimps, krill, squid and small Arctic cod multiply into vast shoals and the sea bed becomes encrusted with shellfish which in turn are fed by the detritus of animals from the surface.

So as we will look out on the desolate snowscape in a few days time when we are aboard the ship and feel sorry for the polar bears who wander this wilderness with no apparent food in sight, we will have to remember that they feed on seal and walrus, who in turn feed on fish and shellfish, who in turn feed on plankton, with the birds picking up the bits on the surface.

So we don't need to feel that any of them will go hungry.

Chapter 3
Getting Ready

Having sorted out the golf club transport problem with Fiona, I had to cross another two hurdles. The first was the not inexpensive problem of getting a visa to enter Russia which from previous experience I knew was an expensive business. Softened to financial spivvery by living in 21st century Britain, even I was not quite ready for the double whammy that was visited upon me when I was told that I had to purchase not one but two Russian visas; this was because I was proposing to sail out of Russia and then-- would you believe it? -- return to Russia. So I had to stump up the fat end of £300 for the pleasure of landing in Russia from a plane, being bussed to a harbour and boarding a ship --- and the reverse on the way back. That came to about £100 for every hour spent in Russia; I suppose that's why they can buy up our soccer teams and houses in Kensington. But that was the game I'd signed up for and translated into the usual language of golf tourism it could be equated to one green fee at Pebble Beach.

The next problem was insuring my aged body. While I did not have any imminent reason to expect my health to break down, the dreaded 'what if' question could not be ignored.

My insurance policy was with my credit card company and so I checked with them before leaving.

'Am I insured for going to the North Pole at my age?'

'Yes. What are you going to do there?'

That was the response that set the alarm bells ringing.

The guy on the other end of the telephone could not have had people my age phone him every day saying what I had said.

"I'm going on a Russian icebreaker"

"OK, but what are you going to do there?"

"What do you mean, what am I going to do there?. I propose to hit a golf ball and take photographs."

"You're not going to ski or dive or paraglide?"

"No."

"Then that's alright. You're insured"

I had not followed the example of most firms that I phone whose automated call system informs me that the telephone conversation would be recorded for 'training purposes'. I wish I had recorded it however because I really didn't believe him, nor did I think that we'd communicated at a level at which his employers would have approved.

What if I got ill? The North Pole is two days' sail through the Barents Sea and two days crashing through ice -- and then some, depending on conditions. There was no possibility of a helicopter ambulance getting that distance north and there was nowhere for a plane to safely land at that time of year. To get an ill person off the boat and back to a hospital would require at least one more ship to sail north and I felt that the person I had spoken to in my telephone conversation had not quite appreciated the risk that he had committed the insurance company to underwrite.

Then my thoughts took on a gloomier side. What if the company who had hired the ice breaker had put conditions in the small print that excused them from all responsibility should someone die. I was so certain that somewhere in that American style small print there would be a 'get out' clause that I never even bothered looking for it because it would have made no difference. I wanted to go, it was on the 'bucket list', and I was on my way.

All the people taking part in the trip had first to get themselves to the Finnish capital, Helsinki. This is a city that lies on a spread of bays, rivers and islands and the metropolitan area is home to one in five Finns. I had fond memories of a previous visit to the city when I received one of the University's medals (I'm not sure what for!). It was February and the temperature was 28 degrees below freezing and the Gulf of Finland, a part of the Baltic Sea, was frozen. On a Sunday, as my wife and I were enjoying the unusual thrill of walking on a frozen sea in cold clean air with no wind and a blue sky, we heard the sound of a choir which was underpinned with the sort of bass voice that is almost unique to the Slavs and Russians. It's unique because God gave some Russian men vocal cords like none other; they are full of a substance that makes them heavier and allows us to enjoy the absolutely unique sound produced by basses such as Feodor Chaliapin.

We traced this particular sound into the Cathedral, which sits atop a hill in the centre of the city and there we found a small circle of Orthodox worshippers singing the Mass all dressed in ankle length fur coats. Unforgettable moments of entranced listening.

But as I landed on this occasion, the cold clear air had been replaced by still warm moist air, like the Scottish Highlands (sometimes), where midges flourish. After a short walk outside the Scandic Hotel (expedition HQ) I returned covered in bites and quite clear in my mind that the rest of my short stay in Finland was going to be indoors.

I had half expected to meet one or two other people from Britain at the airport because we had a fairly short time window for arrival, and flights from London or Amsterdam were not all that frequent. The only person available to share a taxi with me however was a Canadian who was in the paper business and he spent the whole journey complaining about the trouble he continually has from the heavily unionised Finnish paper industry. To a North American that could have meant anything from the Union demanding that the plants close on Christmas Day to demanding shorter hours and more pay. I didn't enquire whether or not he voted Republican but I had my suspicions.

The instructions that had been sent to us suggested that after check-in, we should turn up at the Tour Company desk in the lobby of the hotel. I found this with no difficulty and was soon talking with Greg, a Geology Professor from Minnesota, and Bob, a cheerful bearded academic from the Scott Polar Institute in

Cambridge. After the usual check-in procedures of passport etc I indicated that I was carrying golf clubs, which had been agreed (I didn't mention the struggle) with my agent in England. I had thought that taking golf clubs to the North Pole might be fairly unusual even to seasoned polar voyagers as these two seemed to be, but they seemed totally disinterested. I might as well have volunteered the information that I had brought along my teddy bear with whom I hoped to share my bed. I started to mumble about creating a golf tournament with the hope that this might get them to volunteer some information that other passengers had talked of golf but such was their disinterest that it was obvious that I was not talking to golfers. They either thought I was deranged or had no idea what I'd signed up for, and so any further conversation on the topic of golf became superfluous.

The only issue they were interested in was whether or not the clubs would be regarded as a security risk to the carrier that had been chartered to fly us to Murmansk in Russia where the icebreaker was waiting. They were very fair however and told me I was free to take them but their confiscation would be at my own risk. I was obviously not talking to people who were either familiar with nor sympathetic to, the game of golf; but that did not surprise me.

Greg came from Minnesota which lay north of the State of Iowa where I had spent some of my working life. Golf was impossible there from November through May because of snow, and for the rest of the year, when the courses were open, it was uncomfortably hot and humid.

As for Bob from Cambridge -- well, while one could imagine him being excellent cheerful company at the fireside of a Fens Pub, he just didn't seem to be a 'golf person'.

I enquired of Bob and Norm whether there were any other Brits on the trip and what the spread of nationalities was.

They had obviously not given a lot of thought to this because as they went through the passenger manifest they seemed genuinely surprised that half the names seemed to be Asian. It turned out that indeed almost exactly fifty per cent of the passengers were Chinese computer shop owners who had exceeded their targets of selling more Letmosov lap-top computers that their rivals, and this was their 'bonus' trip. Great!

Of the rest, half were American, and being one of the small band of Brits who actually like Americans, that neither surprised nor disappointed me. It turned out that apart from a guy with a Russian name who lived in London and sold houses to other Russians, I seemed to be the only person from the UK other than Bob; and to define it a little more narrowly, the only member of Bruntsfield Links Golfing Society or the R&A. The remaining 25 passengers were from 15 other countries few of which had a golfing pedigree and so recruiting for a tournament at this point looked to be as much of a challenge as selling a winter holiday in Wigan; but I relaxed with the thought that it was early days yet.

I asked who my cabin companion would be and nearly fainted when the answer came back , Mohammed Al-Bakr. I thought that I knew the Middle East quite well having visited Saudi Arabia, Egypt and Kuwait on many occasions as a consultant, but it was stretching my cultural imagination to its limit to imagine why a rich Saudi boy would want to travel alone in the company of infidels, with no chance of escape, for over two weeks. I could imagine the situation when such a character would 'dip his toe' in such a trip by flying to the pole, but for him to voluntarily commit himself to a voyage of no escape was a new concept to me. Furthermore I was going to have to share a tiny cabin with this chap and I strongly suspected that he was going to pray several times a day and that one of those sessions would be at around 4am.

I also appreciated that when you lived in constant sunshine and heat, the thought of a spell in the cold is as attractive as the opposite is for ourselves. I remembered the well- used ice rinks and artificial ski slopes I'd seen in many Arabian countries.

So why was he going?

Before I had the pleasure of meeting Mohammed I had to spend a night in the hotel with another roommate. This time it was Bryan who was even older than me, having actually entered his ninth decade. He was one of these American surgeons who will continue going to the office and work until the day he dies-- or a patient dies, resulting in an expensive law suit. Retirement from medical practice is something I've never really understood. I retired from surgical practice when I was 61. I had, to all intents and purposes, perfect eyesight, but knew that it wasn't perfect enough for the sort of surgery I did. I used to be able to see the open mouth of blood vessels 3 millimetres wide and was able to clip the forceps on with exactitude. But in the last few years the open mouths of the vessels were not quite as sharp as they used to be and the forceps 'just' missed on the first snatch.

There are some medical specialists who (if they keep their marbles) actually get better the longer they work. For example a radiologist gets more experienced with every X-ray or scan he sees, and like judges, they could safely go on (subject to regular 'marble' checks) until their mid seventies. On the other hand, any practitioner who has to use eye-hand co-ordination, such as a surgeon or an interventional radiologist, should give up well within normal retirement age and concentrate on giving advice from their long experience. I have however kept in touch with many of my former colleagues working outside the UK in the 16 years since I retired and I am astonished at the number who are continuing to work.

I've often thought about this and wondered if they or I have got it wrong. I've come to the conclusion that they continue to work for one of three reasons. Either they still need money to pay College fees or alimony, or they have complete lack of imagination (likely showing they have gone through their entire professional career never having had a sideways thought or another interest) or they have the need for status (doctors have status but it rapidly diminishes when you admit to being deskilled).

I didn't share the room with Bryan for long enough to decide into which category he fell and had we opened the conversation he might not have had time to tell me because he seemed constantly to be dissolving powders. When I asked (I figured it was safe to do so because class A drugs do not come in pretty colours) he told me that as a vegan he had to constantly take food and vitamin supplements to stay healthy. And healthy he was because he probably had less than 1% fat on his skinny frame and had run more marathons than I had had good rounds of golf.

The next morning at 4am we were all wakened, given a bun and coffee, and put on a bus to the clinically clean Helsinki airport. OK, it was early morning and the days' human traffic was still to come, but you could have eaten a meal off the floor at that airport. Why are the Scandinavians so clean? Why don't we live in clinically clean surroundings?

I had plenty of time to consider that and much else, because our charter flight was not leaving for another couple of hours. We were bound for Murmansk on the northern tip of Russia, the place where the Arctic convoys brought cheer to 'Uncle Joe' Stalin during the Second World War.

The other thing I had time to ponder on, was identifying if any of my fellow passengers looked like golfers. Not surprisingly none of them carried golf clubs but that meant little and was not unexpected; after all we'd paid for the Arctic experience, to see wild life, to take photographs of ice and to be able to say that we'd been to the North Pole.

Since I was on my own (my wife had said she would pay not to go on the trip), it was easy to walk up to people, introduce myself, mention St Andrews and then on the basis of their response, which would inevitably mention golf, be able to probe for their interest.

In Scotland, golf is the preserve of the common man, especially in Fife, where, if you don't play, it is a condition treated with both sympathy and concern. When I first moved to St Andrews, I went to order morning newspapers and before the newsagent noted my address he asked, 'D'ye play golf?

'Yes, sort of.'

'Whit's yer handicap?"

'Eighteen,' I replied shamefacedly.

'Never mind. Now you're here, ye'll get better.'

But not being a 'native' of St Andrews I realised that not everyone in the world played golf. J K Rowling invented that wonderful word 'Muggle' which was used by the pupils of Hogwart's to identify a non-magician. I only wish she would invent another word to describe a person who doesn't play golf in St Andrews; it would be tremendously useful.

While it's easy to identify a rugby player or a basketball player from their height and build, it's difficult to tell a golfer. Yes, all the best golfers one sees nowadays on TV seem to be tall, muscular and slim but the ordinary club member can have any shape. Sometimes in an airport lounge one can observe a bored golfer placing his hands in the classic overlap position and then adjusting the position of the knuckle of the index finger or the angle of the V between the thumb and index finger, and sometimes one notices a similarly bored golfer, who, while standing or stretching, might incorporate a swish with his hands and forearms adjusting the position of both during the back and forward swing.

But this cohort of my future companions for the next two weeks seemed either bored, tired or interested in something other than golf. Would 'Guggles' describe them?

Since I was the only one with clubs, one or two people approached me. One such couple was Don and Shirley from South Carolina. To my delight I discovered that they had arrived a day early in Helsinki in order to play the golf course. Wonderful! Another set of 'golf course collectors'. Neither had a very low handicap but they'd worked their way round 18 holes the previous day with hired clubs. I had been on that golf course but not to play golf -- I cross-country skied -- and have never seen the turf.

Don and Shirley were immediately enthusiastic about the prospect of playing in a golf tournament at the North Pole but Shirley was left handed; and when I say left handed I mean that her right side was not connected to her brain. God had given her a right side only for symmetry and as a companion for the all-powerful left. Could she play with right handed clubs? Since there was no hope of getting left handed ones, the game girl said she'd try. But we had a week to sort that out.

I heard two elderly gentlemen speaking Italian and so after introducing myself to Gian Carlo and Maurizio I enquired about their golf skills: they were obviously rich Italians, and since only rich people play golf in Italy I did have some hope that they might throw their hats into the ring. But the response of, 'I'm sorry, we don't play. but we're glad you speak Italian' at least bode for pleasant company for the rest of the trip. Perhaps I could find a role for them on the Organising Committee or, as I decided to call it, in reverence to the R&A, the Championship Committee.

The expedition company had chartered a rather posh Finnair 737 to fly us to Murmansk. Before leaving I'd read Richard Woodman's *Arctic Convoys 1941-44,* a book that had left me chilled at the conditions in which those sailors had had to work in. I'm glad that the few men still alive have at last been recognised and given medals for what they did. I remain amazed that people who took part in these convoys could thereafter lead normal lives, but of more immediate concern was that I got the very clear impression that the Barents Sea was very rough and I was going to have to suffer two days of it. I knew that the worst days of the Arctic convoys had been in the winter but I had taken the precaution of arming myself with every possible seasickness medication.

As we were flying to Russia enjoying a very ample cooked breakfast, Greg, whom I could see was going to be a bundle of unsmiling gloom, warned us to fill up our customs and landing forms without forgetting to dot every 'i' and cross every 't', comforting us with the fact that the Russian customs officials were such bastards that if they found an incorrect entry they might confiscate our belongings either on the way in or on the way out and perhaps even throw us into a Gulag if the month had an 'r' in it!

No such fates overtook us and in fact had I wanted to import a nuclear device to Murmansk it would have been entirely possible, the security was so lax. On driving round the city one could see why there was a reluctance to enforce security. It is the place God forgot.

I have seen poor country villages in Laos and Burma where there is no obvious wealth but people smile, are well dressed and one could imagine some sort of life being possible. I have been in South African townships. I have walked through roadside slums in Mumbai and have been in country villages in Zimbabwe, but I've never seen anywhere like Murmansk.

If I lived there, the most appropriate sound-track to my life would be the theme from the television series *Mash* -- Suicide is Painless!

Chapter 4
Meeting Mohammed

Murmansk is a large-scale slum built of concrete blocks from three different Soviet eras.

The first apartment design dates from Stalin's immediate post-war period and the buildings look exactly as you might imagine a square block would look like if built from old grey Leggo pieces with dark flat roofs rather than red tiles. While there are few worse examples of brutal architecture, we have to understand the reason why Stalin had these built in double quick time.

After what Russia calls the Great Patriotic War and we call World War 2, there were millions of Russians facing death from hypothermia unless they were housed in the few months between the end of the war and winter setting in. For Stalin it was vital that he got as many of the homeless under cover as soon as possible or else there might have been yet another awful human tragedy to add to the unbearable suffering the Russians had endured during the war years. Cramming as many people as possible into a small space meant that each individual was allotted only 4 square metres. More than one family would live in a room, separated by a curtain, and they would share the one toilet and one kitchen which were on each floor with dozens of other families.

It reminded me of the visit to England of a Russian Professor of Surgery in the late eighties.

Each year, in partnership with a colleague, I used to run a course in surgery which became internationally famous and each year we would divert some of the profits towards paying the expenses of a surgeon from an Eastern European country who could not otherwise have afforded it. That particular year the course was being held in Liverpool, where my colleague lived in a Victorian brick pile beside a railway line. It was certainly not the sort of house you would have expected a professor of surgery in a large teaching hospital to live in, but my colleague lived by his political views and did no private practice. However, the property certainly impressed our Russian friend, who stepped back from the front door on his arrival, looked side to side and up and down and in a very admiring tone, said,

'This is enormous. How many families live here?'

One can therefore be sympathetic to the fact that these old Stalinist blocks had not withstood 70 or so winters in the sub-Arctic well. There were broken boarded-up windows, shutters hanging off their hinges, newspapers or blankets acting as curtains and cracks in the concrete that were large enough to admit a hand.

The next era was described as the Krushchev period but I could see little difference apart from the fact that where there once had been cladding on the buildings, most of it had now fallen off leaving exposed breeze block which looked mightily porous. There were those however who had tried to brighten the picture with graffiti; not the artistic designs so frequently seen on the approach to many European railway stations or masterpieces by Banksy, but Cyrillic letters which were obviously expressing the love that one young Murmansk boy/girl had for another, or an unintelligible phrase denoting some dissatisfaction with the police or government.

One would have expected the third generation of flats, those from the Brezhnev era, to be the best. Wrong! These were in fact the most awful. The seventies, especially in Europe, was not a golden period of architecture and that applies especially to buildings commissioned by a State no matter which. In our country we need only think of income tax offices, social security offices and employment exchanges built in that era. But even the worst excesses of brutalism that deface our cities here in Britain were Greco-Roman classics compared to what the Russians built in those years. These had no cladding, lots of cracks, broken windows, hanging shutters and no sign of humans. But there was graffiti.

Murmansk in a cold drizzle on midsummer's day looked as God had intended -- a place one step away from Hell. To me it looked like a place that people were sent rather than a place to which people went and we were subsequently told by our guide that that indeed was the case. If you did volunteer to go there, you could get a little more money, pay a little less tax and receive more generous benefits. So it might have been better than living in a doorway on a Moscow street.

Having been woken at 4am, the day was passing slowly in this monument to depressive Stalinist Russia, but we were eventually told that the reason for being apparently imprisoned in a bus was that we had to wait until 4pm for the tide to change so that we could leave -- and if we missed that tide we could not leave before 4am the next day. This I found a little disconcerting because our ship, the *50 Years of Victory,* had been announced to us as the world's most powerful nuclear ice breaker which would smash it's way through whatever ice lay between us and the North Pole and so to have such a monster having to wait for such an old fashioned concept as a mere tide was somehow difficult to understand.

Earlier in the day they had taken us to a similar ship which was now a museum. It was called *The Lenin* and was no longer in service. We were looking forward to having a preview of the sort of ship that was to be our home for the next two weeks, but the atmosphere became a little more anxious when an elderly Swiss physicist asked the guide if this was the ship that had had the nuclear accident some years ago with some fatal consequences! The guide, of course, denied any knowledge of any such event but in situations like this I always find it safer to trust elderly Swiss physicists.

In Murmansk you have few alternatives other than to do what you are told. If you don't, there is always the possibility that they might leave you there, and this is not an acceptable option. So we continued with the longest bus tour I've ever experienced. As the guide was running out of things to show us she directed the bus up an enormous hill from where we could see the massive harbours of the city. The top of the hill was dominated by the biggest lump of raw concrete that I'd ever seen. It was in the shape of a Russian soldier and while not being clear as to what it represented I'm sure that at one time it

Golf at the North Pole

had provided many local people with a job; it was a great pity they did not employ a designer.

As lunchtime passed and the afternoon wore on with no mention of food I realised why we'd had such a slap-up breakfast on the charter plane at what seemed like an age ago. I was hungry but I had seen no restaurants in our never ending drive around Murmansk. Norm added to the cheer with a constant running commentary about the difficulty he anticipated from the Russian customs officials at the docks who, if they were not feeling co-operative or one of us smiled, might take it into their heads to delay us even further.

Fortunately the brown envelopes must have contained satisfactory contributions to their widows and orphans fund because we went straight through with no security checks at all.

And that set me thinking again about why a chap called Mohammed was sailing with us. In these days when we are brainwashed into regarding every Islamist as a potential terrorist and at regular intervals in UK we read about some or other potential atrocity being uncovered by our secret service, the thought of a chap called Mohammed going to the North Pole without any security check did set some alarm bells ringing in my head. In Helsinki I'd made some sort of feeble attempt at a joke with Norm by suggesting that I might be first out of the boat if a bomb went off in my cabin (he didn't laugh) but I must say I was looking forward to meeting Mohammed and getting my peace of mind back.

Had I not previously seen photographs of what was to be home for the next two weeks I would have been shocked at my first sight of the ship. It had a large rounded bow and stern but there seemed to be far more on top than there was below. Topping the deck was a monstrously large rusty red steel block with windows. It looked like a pile of freight containers on a cargo vessel but behind one of these windows was a cabin that was to be my home for the next two weeks.. However I'd read all about the previous polar expeditions and if they could survive a winter in a snow house on cracking ice surrounded by polar bears I felt that I could steel myself to withstand two weeks in the Arctic summer in this vessel.

I was shown into Cabin 85, which fortunately was on the same deck level as the reception area and the dining room, but that was the best that could be said of it. Literally, there wasn't room to swing a cat. There were two windows on one wall and from door to window the length was about four metres; if I stood in the middle of the cabin with both arms outstretched I wasn't too far short of touching both walls.

Under the windows was a couch that turned into a bed at night and the only proper bunk bed was on one wall lengthwise. Opposite it, on the other wall, was a shelf-like desk topped by a large mirror and towards the door, abutting the desk/shelf was a thin wardrobe with minimal space. Between the wardrobe and the door was a half metre space into which you were supposed to compress and store your luggage. To be fair to the company, they had made a big point of telling us that any luggage should be carried in soft compressible bags and now I could see why.

On the right side of the door was the smallest bathroom I'd ever seen, but it proved to be adequate provided you sat on the loo before having a shower and flooding the entire floor.

And I was going to have to share this space with Mohammed for 14 nights.

Mohammed had obviously collected his luggage and had arrived in the cabin before me because there were a couple of bags on the floor.

The immediate problem, as I got my bearings, was the issue of 'the bed'. I stowed my luggage and unpacked my books onto the bed, waiting to see what would happen when my companion appeared. I waited and waited, trying to anticipate any other problems that could arise through sharing a small space. But my mind kept drifting back to my assertion that I was sharing this space with a Saudi Arabian called Mohammed who was probably going to pray several times a day and I just could not see how the cabin would cope . . . unless he was tiny.

When Mohammed finally appeared, he was no midget. Towering over me at well over six feet and weighing something around the 250 lbs mark, Mohammed was a giant.

While sitting on the only bed, I rushed to suggest that I would sleep there on the way to the North Pole and he could use it on the way back. He was half my age and, with the impeccable respect that Arabs have for the elderly, he demurred, saying that he would be fine sleeping on the couch and I could have the bed on the way up as well as the way back.

Since I wasn't sure of the policy or costs for buying alcoholic drinks, I had taken the precaution of buying a bottle of the finest Finnish vodka at Helsinki airport, but in order not to offend Mohammed I obviously had to keep it hidden. I knew several Saudi gentlemen who could hold their own with locals in the Big Room at the R&A but I also remembered being told by a Saudi doctor that alcohol was 'Satan's vomit'. So one always had to be sensitive to the issue.

Unlike the rest of the passengers (apart from the Chinese computer shop owners on their bonus trip), Mohammed was young. He told me that he was 34 and was 'in construction'. Probing further I found that he was the youngest son of the Saudi family, distantly related to royalty, who did most of the major works both in Jeddah and in Riyadh.

I enquired why he was going to the North Pole and his answer floored me. He said he was going to the highest point of the world in order to pray. He wanted to be as close to God as possible when he sent up his prayer.

I was going to be sharing a space smaller than my home downstairs WC with someone who was spending a lot of money in order to kneel in the snow at 90 degrees north in order to pray.

My throat became dry.

"Why," I was able to croak out.

He told me his story.

Just as religion was driven out of Silvio Berlusconi's soul by being educated by Silesian monks in Milan, so Mohammed left school and University more in love with the secular life than with the teachings of the Prophet. Although he qualified from university with an engineering degree and was an important cog in the family construction firm, he, like many other wealthy Saudi boys, looked to the fleshpots of the world rather than the ascetic life. I didn't probe into his favourite type of debauchery, but I mentally classified his previous life under 'Sex, Drugs and Rock 'n Roll'.

But, again like many Saudi rich boys, either he 'saw the light' or the light was shown to him. Last year he had performed Hajj and had travelled to Mecca where he 'found' God. Since that point he had been very holy.

Just as I had been collecting golf courses all my life, he was starting his own collection, of unique places from which to pray.

I was very relieved to hear his story. Given my own reason for visiting the Pole, his seemed equally logical. I was very relieved that I wouldn't have to protect myself during the night from an obvious 'nutter'.

Although it wasn't Ramadan, Mohammed ate very little, only having breakfast and nothing else during the day. While the rest of us were lunching and dining, he took himself off to the crew's quarters and joined in games of basketball and volleyball (to such an extent that when we were disembarking the crew gave him the award for 'most popular passenger'). Not that any of the other passengers could have matched his fitness or energy, the next youngest being 30 years older than him.

At 90 degrees North the only direction is south, so I asked Mohammed how he would know which direction to face when we arrived at the Pole. There would be no possibility of pointing east... but the boy had thought it through.

'I shall pray looking upwards,' he said. 'At that point no one will be closer to God than me in the whole world.'

Well, it takes all sorts.

Chapter 5
Passengers And Crew

Four distinct groups sailed to the North Pole aboard *50 years of Victory* . They were the Crew, the Hotel staff, the Expedition staff and the passengers.

The crew was Russian. When they are leading convoys through the seas on the north Russian coastline they live in the cabins that have been allotted to us-- but with one difference-- one crew member to a cabin! I could understand the tour company squashing us in but to charge twice for a single use cabin suggests that some of them had served an apprenticeship in the City of London at some time in their lives. The crew has conditions of employment that are far removed from my impressions of what life on the ocean wave was about-- especially a Russian ocean wave.

They had the use of a small swimming pool, a court that could be used for volley ball, basketball and badminton, and two saunas. At certain times, these facilities were reserved for passengers, but few in their seventh or eighth decades trod the boards of the activities court other than young Mohammed.

When we had a tour of the ship it seemed that their days were spent looking at computer screens monitoring the functions of power, radioactivity and desalination. At one point during the tour, our guide held up a board that said we were 9 metres below the water line; she held up a board because the machines around us were so noisy that speech was impossible. There was also a radio officer who sat in a capacious salon which housed the telephones and internet connections but these cost a great deal of money to use.

Then there were the hotel crew; largely Austrian with a few Russians. They were absolutely terrific and seemed to be working round the clock. The meals were of the highest quality and there were two cuisines. One of course was European but because of the 50 Chinese passengers there was always Chinese food available for breakfast, lunch and dinner.

The first day was a bit of a disaster because the staff had not anticipated the hunger of the Chinese. It would be quite incorrect to assume that I imply greed, but the nutritional action stations taken by the Chinese on the first day was a little surprising. If you followed a Chinese person to the buffet there would be nothing left-- either Chinese or European. I was left asking myself, if I felt hungry for most of our day in Murmansk, how must they have felt? But the Austrians quickly saw what was wrong and sorted it by the second day.

I've always admired the Austrians; a country that can convince the world that Hitler was a German and

Golf at the North Pole

Beethoven was an Austrian, must contain some very clever people.

The third group on board were the expedition crew.

Basically there was a tour leader, three lecturers, a helicopter pilot, a hot air balloon pilot, a girl who sold expensive polar bear knick-knacks and tee shirts in the shop, and four guys doing what was generously called 'logistics', which really meant doing anything that required to be done.

Among the 'logistic experts' were Bill, an office worker from headquarters in Toronto who was getting a 'freebie' probably as a bonus, Roger, an English drifter who lectured on ornithology and photography, and Andrew, a Canadian whose construction firm hit the buffers in the recession and was obviously several leagues of intelligence ahead of the others.

These guys were all 'normal'. They had jobs and skills and one could see all of them eventually becoming successful in whatever direction they chose to go. But not Burt. He came from Oregon, had graduated from High School and had got into College. He'd studied Engineering but quickly found that the world of academia was not for him. He set off on the 'journey of life' and his first port of call was Disneyland, where he became a waiter on roller skates. Had he been Scottish, his granny would have been disappointed in him at this stage. She would have been much prouder of him when he went to Wall Street where he became a trader. I suppose in the circumstances of our time we always associate 'trading' with success but we would be wrong. Burt was an unsuccessful trader and went back to roller skating but when the opportunity came to crew polar trips he jumped at the chance. And he was good at it; a court jester supreme, who made everyone laugh and was excellent company. But his granny would still have been unhappy.

The tour leader, Laurie Dexter, was a unique man of the Arctic. Over breakfast one morning he told me his story.

Born in the Shetland Isles some 60 years previously he had been brought up in a house which had neither electricity nor television. His heroes were the Shetlanders who had been away on whaling expeditions and had returned with stories of the polar regions. That stimulated his imagination to such an extent that he decided to work where there were extremes of ice and cold. I admired his fertile imagination to realise that there were places colder than Shetland.

But he was not to remain in Shetland for long. His parents took him south to Glasgow, where he devoured books about the Arctic and Antarctic, which were plentifully available from the Mitchell library. Not having distractions such as television or computer games, the more he read the more he 'knew' that the snow and ice were to be his preferred future environment.

When his parents decided to emigrate to Canada, he was delighted because it gave him a gateway to the wilderness. As a very fit sports-minded young man, he did a degree in physical education and was teaching this subject when he read in a newspaper that the Anglican Church was going to open the biggest parish in the world on Baffin Island.

That's where Laurie wanted to go and so he went to the Archbishop and asked how he could get the job of ministering to that Inuit community.

An astonished Archbishop pointed out to him that there would be three hurdles to clear. The first was that he should become an Anglican, the second was that he needed a theology degree and the third was that he had to train as an Anglican priest! This might have been too much for some, but not Laurie. He did all of these things, got the job and took his family to Baffin Island, where, for the next 13 years, he ran the biggest parish in the world, having a wonderful time visiting his five churches by aeroplane, snowmobile, dog sled and zodiac. While in the North he learned survival skills from his Inuit parishioners and did various expeditions, gradually gathering the experience needed to enter the first league of exploring.

When he left Baffin Island, he continued with his expedition work until he got into the premier league of explorers and was invited to join a Russian-Canadian expedition that planned to ski from Canada to Russia over the North Pole, a trip that would take 91 days.

As part of the team that succeeded in this, he received decorations both from Canada and Russia.

As a sideline, he did ultra marathons. On his curriculum, he listed having run ten marathons in ten days, 100Km in 8 hours, 200Km in 24 hours and 600Km in 6 days.

We felt safe with Laurie leading us.

I asked him about golf, but he denied ever having played, though I was sure that he could probably have reached a single figure handicap had he practised for a few weeks!

Laurie was actually the only person to wear a tie at the introductory reception; it was a bow tie, worn with such gaucheness that one saw quite clearly it was not part of Laurie's everyday gear.

While Laurie looked a bit at sea at the introductory party at least one couple had come very well prepared. Bob, a former American newspaper owner and now a philanthropist had brought a tuxedo with a black-edged white evening shirt and patent leather shoes. The rest of us looked like 'trailer park trash' compared to him and his beautiful wife.

The other group that stood apart from us did so because of a language barrier. I didn't meet a single one of the 50 Chinese passengers who spoke English and so there were really two distinct groups and I'm sure each muttered about the foibles of the other. It was a shame because they did seem pretty jolly and enormously polite-- but distanced.

I used to do facelifts when I had a day job, at a time when the procedure did not only take four hours but was also a very unsatisfying operation. The new techniques, with which I am not familiar, are much better and I could see from looking round that almost every American woman on board had had one. I could see the imperfections of the job quite easily and so, rather like being on a safari and ticking off the animals, I was able to comment on the excellence or otherwise of the facelifts much to the enjoyment of Gian Carlo and Maurizio.

It was while I was waiting with them for our helicopter flight that I met 'call me Ginger'.

I was waiting with my two Italian friends for the fourth person to join us on our helicopter flight when a very good looking, mature lady came along. The introduction was Californian who introduced herself with a 'Call me Ginger' (I think her name was Virginia but I may be wrong) and she seemed delighted to be in the company of Italians. Her first statement was 'I drive Italian cars'.

As the owner of an Alfa Romeo I enquired if we drove similar models. Her reply was in the negative. 'I have a Ferrari, a Maserati and two Lamborghinis,' she said.

This was someone from another world. She added that she flew to Europe for every Grand Prix and sponsored a US driver with one of the main marques.

In the first few days of the trip the e-mail facility was occupied 24/7 by her two teenage sons who looked as if they were doing 'cold turkey' away from the internet. Well they weren't quite 'cut off' because money seemed to be no object, but at a dollar a minute most of us lay low; if however you can afford to take two teenagers on a trip like this then what's a few hundred more to let the boys communicate with their girlfriends.

Ginger was a charming lady rumoured to be an heiress to a major American company. Certainly to take two teenagers on a trip like this did suggest a certain financial status.

Not every passenger however seemed to be as rich as Bob and Ginger. Some Europeans seemed as relatively poor as myself and while most of the other Americans must have been wealthy few showed it. I really liked the elderly lady from California who told me about her mission to save as many 'Mom' cats and their litters as possible. She obviously had a huge house because she had a room each for the 'Mom' and her litter. She would have the veterinarian do all the health checks and she herself would put would-be owners through a strict screening before allowing one of her cats to go to a new home.

When we were introduced to the expedition crew, there was a special introduction for the two barmen-- Stefan and Wolfgang -- both of whom had their own bars in Vienna and who were obviously enjoying a 'freebie' to the North Pole; two delightful characters who were fluent in English and expert in cocktails. Every day there was a new cocktail almost always on a vodka base.

My favourite was a simple one called Arctic which was vodka and creme-de-menthe but this was closely followed by Ballet Russe -- vodka, black raspberry liqueur, lime juice and sugar syrup. Close runners up were Dyevitchka (vodka, triple sec, pineapple juice, and lime juice), Moscow Mule (vodka, lime juice, ginger beer and angostura bitters) and Raspberry Cobbler (vodka, cranberry juice, lemon juice and raspberries). But the cause of many headaches was Seasonal Breeze which was vodka, cranberry juice and a touch of apple juice. These men were artistes.

As a singleton, I spent a lot of time in the bar with other loners both during the day and after dinner. The bar was situated at the front of the upper deck and we had a wonderful view of the open leads and ice while we 'sipped' the day away. The curved seating arrangement was conducive to large groups getting together although one girl who was writing a book and the Russian house salesman from London always sat apart from larger groups.

I spent many evenings talking to Klaus, a third-generation owner of factories that made bearings for BMW and Volkswagen engines. He was overweight with a frightful past medical history of cardiac problems but was looking forward to signing up for the Virgin spaceflight. I expressed some caution and doubt for a person such as him going into space. First of all I doubted that Virgin would allow a person of this size to occupy two seats and, even though I had been retired for many years, I still had the clinical acumen to doubt if survival from such an experience would be possible for him. I didn't bring up the subject of death however and concentrated on the costs; he seemed to think that a quarter of a million dollars was a reasonable price for such an experience. I'll remember that if I ever buy a German car.

Dennis from California was great fun but probably crazy. He had come to the expedition via Moscow, where he had bought the 'Mig-29 experience'.

Shortly after the Berlin Wall came down, first the Poles, then most of the other former Iron Curtain countries had developed the idea of military 'tourism'. It doesn't come cheap, but you go to a military base, get oriented and instructed and then choose the sort of one hour flight you want. You can do anything from straight line fast flying to full battle manoeuvres. Rob chose the latter, which turned out not to be a wise choice because he doesn't travel well and told us that he spent most of his hour being sick. But he described it as 'fantastic'. He was even given a ball to throw in the air to prove that he was weightless for a time!

On the boat, while everyone else was dressed in sweaters and thick trousers, he walked the corridors in colourful Hawaiian shirts, shorts and USC top.

Anders, a Belgian doctor, was a fellow professional who had spent his life ministering to the local population in the Belgian Congo. He had of course become an expert in tropical diseases and had seen the first cases of AIDS before it had become widespread in the west. He and his colleagues had, for want of a better name, called it 'slim disease' because the affected young man would just go and lie down in his hut, waste away and die -- for, at that time, no apparent reason.

Since he'd retired he'd been on almost perpetual vacation, travelling in the Arctic and Antarctic, and had become expert in his local knowledge, which he transmitted to me most evenings after dinner .

I, together with Don and Shirley who had played golf in Helsinki, spent time planning the golf tournament and trying to recruit anyone who wanted to enter.

Unfortunately the language barrier stopped us approaching 50 per cent of the passengers.

Don had started life as a military man and ended his service career as a navy pilot. He had also met Neil Armstrong, and after I told him that my meeting with Armstrong had been the reason for me wanting to play golf at the North Pole, he asked me if I'd explored the story of Mr Gorky when I'd met him.

I replied in the negative and Don educated me.

Everyone knows that when Armstrong stepped on to the moon, he said, "That's one small step for man, one giant leap for mankind", but apparently as he re-entered the landing craft he was heard in Houston to make the enigmatic and almost inaudible comment, "Good Luck, Mr Gorsky". People at NASA thought it was a casual remark concerning some rival Soviet cosmonaut but when they checked there was no Gorsky in either the Russian or American space programmes. He was asked frequently to explain that remark but always demurred.

Then on July 5th, 1995, in Tampa Bay, Florida, while answering questions following a speech, a young reporter asked him the 26 year old question -- 'Who's Mr Gorsky?'

This time he evidently did respond, because Mr Gorsky was now dead. It turned out that in 1938, when Neil was a kid in a small mid-western town, he was playing baseball with a friend in his back yard when his friend hit the ball into a neighbour's yard under their bedroom window. The property belonged to Mr and Mrs Gorsky and, as he leaned down to pick up the ball,

Neil heard Mrs Gorsky shout at Mr Gorsky, "You want sex! You'll get sex when that kid next door walks on the moon."

Even had I known that story I would never have brought up the taboo subject of sex in the Big Room.

Evan and Grace were a charming couple from Adelaide. He had been a very successful engineer but had never played golf. I found this strange because everyone I've ever met from Adelaide has been a member of the Royal Adelaide Golf Club and many were also members of the R&A with enough wealth to attend the Autumn meeting in St Andrews. I'd once had a trainee from Adelaide who'd gone back to that beautiful town to make his fortune, a thing he'd done so 'successfully' that he was known to every citizen of the City because his trial had been covered in every newspaper. No more will be said.

Then there was Trevor, a New Zealand farmer. He didn't admit to playing regular golf but he looked such a (former) athletic person that I felt sure he would play his part in my prospective tournament. For the entirety of my life, New Zealand have beaten all the British countries at rugby, while giving the appearance of being able to do it with such ease that they might only have needed half the number of men. In recent years the British teams have produced much bigger men thus approaching physical parity with the opposition, but in years gone by the Kiwis seemed to be men from other planets.

Even before professional rugby, with its attendant 'conditioning' producing 'monster men', many of the

Golf at the North Pole

New Zealand rugby players were farmers who were used to carrying a sheep under each arm. This upper body and arm strength made robbing the ball from an effete English public schoolboy extremely easy. When one of these monsters got injured, all the selectors did was to climb the hills, holler for another sheep farmer and the slot would be filled immediately. Trevor came from that era. Hands like shovels, a head like a hydrocephalic and the body shaped like a tank, admittedly now carrying a little extra weight, but one had the impression that two days in a gym would replicate the 1955 model!

And then there were the Italians who were delighted to meet another Italian speaker in Helsinki-- Gian Franco and Maurizio. Former executives in a major Italian Nationalised organisation, they had wives with the same view of going to cold places in June as mine and like mine, had offered to pay not to go.

As I suspected, living part of the year in Italy, this was not an environment for Italians. Over dinner, by the third night they had come to the opinion that their wives had been correct and that this was not the way to spend 15 days in mid-summer.

One of the reasons I choose to live a large part of the year in Italy is the food. For very little you can eat like a prince in small family trattorias and since every Italian lady of a certain age knows how to cook well, they eat even better at home.

Quite simply the fact that there are so few Chinese restaurants in Italy is that the average Italian thinks that this is not food for humans and so the sight and smell of Chinese cuisine at breakfast, lunch and dinner was not found to be too appealing by my friends. Solid Austrian type food was acceptable in small quantities as a substitute for normal Italian nutrition and so meal times became an amusing litany as to the source of what we were eating.

There were many others (apart from the Chinese), but these people became my chosen friends for the two weeks that we spent cruising on the top of the world.

Chapter 6
Sea Sickness

As gloomy Greg forecast, the Russian customs had been very 'picky' -- not with us but with the cargo of merchandise, food and medicines that we were carrying. The expedition company have a policy of always having on board a medical officer who is an American 'Board Certified' Emergency Room Physician; they are very wise. These doctors are trained in all forms of 'front line' medicine and since medicine and surgery is so specialised now, they are just about the only doctors who have the necessary general range of skills to cope with any situation.

Our physician, Ted, was taking a short sabbatical from his main employment at a prestigious Mid-West University Hospital. I questioned him about my fear as to what care someone might receive when out of contact with emergency recovery services. He assured me that he could probably keep anyone alive for the two or three days that would be required for the ship to get close enough for a pick-up. Cruise doctoring had certainly moved on since my day when medical staff onboard were usually unskilled retired GPs on a 'jolly'.

He was obviously carrying a range of medicines that was beyond the expertise of the Murmansk customs officials and they evidently had a strong impression that many of them were either new recreational drugs or some form of 'for profit' contraband.

The delay meant we missed the 4pm tide and we spent a rather uninteresting evening watching the scenery of the Murmansk docks (where it was still raining) and as we slept under what might have been the midnight sun had it not been raining, the ship sailed on the 4am tide.

When I woke up we were moving. I knew we were moving because I saw the horizon and sea moving but the ship was as still as a rock. So much for reading about Arctic convoys, North Atlantic storms and an expensive supply of sea-sickness remedies.

It was going to take us just over two days to sail through the Barents Sea and considering the number of people who were already wearing scopolamine patches behind their ears I was not the only one who had done research on the likely sea conditions . As it was however, although there were plenty of waves with white tops the boat never budged - no doubt due to the deep keel that housed all that nuclear equipment.

Medical textbooks are no more informative now than they were 50 years ago about the mechanism of motion sickness but I have always been impressed by some unpublished research that was going on when I worked in America. It was being done by a former USAF pilot who had been one of the early high-speed jet fighter pilots and who had been a late graduate from medical school and was researching why so many of the new very high -speed jets were crashing on landing -- all rather strangely with the stick pushed forwards, as if the pilot thought he had been too nose-up to land. His name was Kent Gillingham.

He developed the theory of what he called 'sensory incongruity' and later applied it to motion sickness.

One of the functions of the brain is to keep the body 'safe'. The famous French physiologist Claude Bernard used the words *milieu interior,* also known as homeostasis. By this he meant that the brain and nervous system are always attempting to keep the bodily functions working normally no matter the circumstances and that it would react in a reflex manner without you thinking about it. Thus withdrawing your hand on touching a hot object is an example of one of these reflexes that the brain (and not you) controls.

In our inner ears one set of receptors tells us if we are spinning or rotating either forwards or sideways and another set that inform us if we are going forward or back or are upright or upside down. Kent pointed out that if the brain did not damp down these signals it was receiving continually from the inner ears then we would spend our time being dizzy or off balance. Every time we move our heads one receptor or other is stimulated and if you thought you were, say, spinning you would tend to move your body in the opposite direction in order to counter the perceived movement. What the brain therefore does is to teach itself to ignore these received signals. It sort of says "ignore that movement and that signal. We've done it a thousand times and it causes no harm". This is called 'inhibition'.

In other words, when the inner ear is stimulated by mild bodily movement or head movement the signals are damped down before they reach what is called the vestibular nucleus in the brain stem.

Your eyes tell you how you are positioned in regard to whatever moving platform you're in or on, whether it be a boat, a motor car or an aeroplane, or even just walking along the road. If whatever vehicle you are on is bouncing about then the eyes send signals to the brain that assure it that the abnormal movement is OK and the brain need not react.

Let's say you now go onto a boat in a rough sea or an aeroplane that is caught in a thunderstorm and is wobbling about in the sky. These are abnormal movements. Your eyes see that in relation to the fixtures on the boat or the interior of the aeroplane you seem to have a fixed position but the signals from the inner ear are 'strange'. The brain, which is always trying to protect the body from harm says 'this is more than the usual head movements and what's more these signals say 'I'm bobbling about' but the eye signals say 'I'm not'.

This is what Kent Gillingham defined as 'sensory incongruity'-- in other words contradictory messages arriving in the brain.

Let's imagine you, as a person, were in a dangerous situation; what would you want to do? You'd want to get as much information as possible so that you could figure out how to get out of the danger.

That's what the brain does.

It takes off the inhibition that it normally applies to the stream of impulses coming from the inner ear with the result that the vestibular nucleus is bombarded with electrical signals, so much so that when every cell in the vestibular nucleus is filled the electrical impulses start to 'overflow'.

Right next to the vestibular nucleus is what is called the vagal nucleus. This is where one of the main nerves of the body, the vagus nerve, starts from. The vagus nerve supplies among other things the heart, blood vessels, the salivary glands and the stomach.

The vagal nucleus gets taken by surprise by all this electricity pouring into it from the neighbouring vestibular nucleus but doesn't have any idea of why. So it reacts as a vagal nucleus ought to by turning on its connections. And when the vagal nerve is stimulated that is when the symptoms of motion sickness start.

First you get excessive salivation, then you go pale, then you feel nauseous and finally your stomach churns and you're sick. If someone took your pulse at that moment they would find it was slow-- just as it would be in a faint (another vagal episode)-- and because the vagus nerve has narrowed all the blood vessels to the skin you stay pale for many hours after a spell of sickness.

This theory also explains individual differences in proneness to motion sickness. We all know people who board a moving vehicle 'sure' that they will be sick -- and they usually are. What these people are doing is reacting to past experience and virtually telling their brains to 'take off' the inhibition early and so the cycle happens earlier. Others have an anatomical 'separation' between the vestibular nucleus and the vagal nucleus in their brains so that no matter how much information overflows from the vestibular nucleus it has nowhere to go and ends up in the brain's 'no-mans-land' and these lucky people are never sick or even nauseous.

Motion sickness was a problem in early space flight especially in the larger Russian Soyuz spacecraft which were bigger than the American ships. Space craft rotate so they don't get fried by the sun and moving the head in this environment creates an enormous force known as the Coriolis effect and so early American astronauts stayed as still as possible and instrument readings did not involve much head movement.

Then the 'trainers' realised what was what and set up training schemes that involved teaching the brain that crazy sensory incongruity was 'normal' and that no matter what impulses came into the brain stem the top of the brain should not 'panic' and take off inhibition. Thus trainee astronauts have to spend many hours in rotating centrifuges to train their brains that 'sensory incongruity' is 'normal'.

There are no drugs that prevent motion sickness. Kent Gillingham created dizziness in cats while they had electrodes in their vestibular nuclei. He could thus measure the signals arriving there and could thus test the effects of drugs in diminishing that signal. The only one to diminish the signal and thus lessen the chance of the brain 'taking off' the normal inhibition was valium. But the dosage was such that you would sleep deeply through any storm. Other drugs such as scopolamine or antihistamines only attempt to counteract the symptoms once the vagal nucleus has been stimulated.

But thank goodness, the Barents Sea was like a mill-pond.

Chapter 7
Eskimos And Myths

As I woke on the first morning, Mohammed was already up, probably having prayed a couple of times since we last spoke, and he was reading about the Arctic - in Arabic (a minority market).

'I wonder if we'll see any Eskimos' he said.

'You can't say that word Mohammed. In the Arctic to call the people who live here Eskimos is the equivalent of using the 'N' word'.

'Tell me what is this 'N' word'

I didn't know the chap very well and I felt that this was not going to be a line of conversation that would lead to close bonding.

'Mohammed, I've no idea why Eskimos don't like that word being used to describe them but I don't like to be called a Jock, you don't like to be called a Raghead and African Americans don't like to be called 'N.....s'-- that's the 'N' word.

'Well I don't understand that because plenty of people hate us Arabs and I know that African Americans are discriminated against but the Eskimos are lovely people. We see pictures of them standing outside their igloos dressed in furs looking after their beautiful white dogs. What do they want to be called?'

'Inuits' I said.

'That's a crazy name. Why not something spectacular like 'Icemen' or 'Northman'?'

I told him that the official change came in 1977 at the Inuit Circumpolar Conference meeting in Barrow, Alaska when it became official that they wanted the term *Inuit* used as a designation for all circumpolar native peoples. As a result the Canadian government officially abandoned the word *Eskimo* which was considered pejorative.

Before he'd come, Mohammed had read about the ancient Greek astronomer and geographer Pytheas, who lived in the Greek province of Massilia (Marseilles). He told me about him.

Pytheas must have been a very brave man with an even braver crew because he did the unthinkable and sailed out of the safety of the known world of the time -- the Mediterranean. Apparently no one had ever done that before and so his exit, especially using what we would now reckon were primitive vessels, was even more remarkable. He went through the Straits of Gibraltar, which, to early Greek sailors was a kamikaze manoeuvre, and he was never expected to be seen again. His voyage took place around 330 BC and is said to have lasted about

6 years. The reason he left the safety of the known world was to search for sources of tin and amber.

He turned left at one point and found the tin mines of Cornwall but didn't then turn right to enter the Baltic and so missed the source of amber. He continued North to investigate a land called Thule, where he had been told that the sun was visible at midnight at the time of the summer solstice. Another days' sail north of Thule saw him meet an 'impenetrable element where the sea, earth and sky, congealed into a single mass' -- by which he must have meant Ice.

Even before that the Greeks had had some theories about what was going on in the world north of their idyllic blue skies and seas. While their world was centred on the Mediterranean, they did however realise that life to the north and east of the Balkan mountains was pretty rugged and much colder than around the Mediterranean.

They thought there were probably a nomadic people called Scythians and and a simple extrapolation of this led them to suppose that the Scythian land was bounded to the North by the impenetrable 'Riphean mountains' (which were probably an amalgamation of the Carpathian, Caucasus and Altai ranges). In the Greek winter, when the cold wind blew from the North it came to be known as the Boreas and not surprisingly the Greek wise men (early meteorologists) thought that the Boreas emanated from a cave in the Riphean Mountains -- but they never wrote down exactly where that cave was.

The concept was expanded when some seer put forward the idea that there might even be people living north of the Scythians. It gradually became accepted that this mythical people who lived north of the Riphean mountains were the 'Hyperboreans'. This mythical group was also considered to be the most fortunate people on the Earth because they lived in a fantastic climate in which there were no seasons, with their trees bearing fruit all the year round. The Hyperboreans devoted their lives to music, dance, serenity and comfort; they did not need to work and they lived in a disease-free environment. Even better, they were supposed to be immortal with their ultimate destiny lying in their own hands. It was said that when they had lived for about 1000 years and were perhaps getting bored with their blissful existence, they would end it by throwing themselves off a cliff into the ocean.

But that story sparked enough interest for me to go to the ship's library to learn more about the mythology of the 'North'.

The location of 'Thule', the place that Pytheas found, has been the subject of much debate for 2000 years and variously, it has been identified as the west coast of Norway, the south coast of Iceland or somewhere north of the Shetland Isles. It was however, a useful landmark for contemporary map makers because from the time that the concept of the imaginary Thule was accepted, all unknown territory in the North was named *'Ultima Thule'*.

It was not until the nineteenth century that Thule got a permanent position. That was when a Danish geographer used the name for the site of the most northerly Inuit population in Greenland. Two thousand years after Pytheas had been there, the Americans built a huge air base for surveillance during the Cold War!

In the middle ages, as Christianity spread north, mapping became more accurate, but still the very top of the world remained *Ultima Thule.* Perhaps the best map of the time was created by the Flemish geographer Gerhard Mercator whose 1569 map served many explorers including Martin Frobisher and other early Arctic explorers.

The extraordinary belief that the Arctic was a place of Hyperborean ecstasy was slow to disappear and it was only as the tales of the early explorers became more widely known that the concept started to be disbelieved.

But what beliefs remained were resurrected by Friedrich Nietzsche in his 1895 essay *The Antichrist,* in which he compared the northern supermen of Hyperborean peoples of the Arctic with degenerate southern Europeans. And this was before casino banking and tax evasion had been invented!

In 1912 the Thule Society was formed in Germany and it propounded the theory that the island of Thule had been a northern Atlantis, home to an advanced civilisation, and had mysteriously been destroyed by an unknown disaster. They wanted to recreate this Order of Aryan supermen who would eventually exterminate the inferior races of the world and they were one of the many progenitors of Hitler's National Socialist Party of the early 1920s.

The myths were also kept alive by various writers of the nineteenth century such as Mary Shelley, who, in her

1816 story *Frankenstein,* described a place where snow and ice were banished by the sun being forever visible, *'it's broad disk just skirting the horizon and diffusing a perpetual splendour"*

We know that if snake oil is sold as a universal cure of disease with great marketing skill then people will buy it, but I still find it hard to believe that a former American Army officer, John Cleves Symmes was able to sell his theory of the Poles at the beginning of the nineteenth century.

By peddling his view of 'alternative geography' he made a lot of money lecturing to packed houses all over America. The theory that he sold at the beginning of the nineteenth century was based on his belief that the broad entrances at the North and South Poles gave access to the habitable interior of the Earth. As he lectured he used a huge wooden globe with countersunk holes at each end to represent what he had christened 'Symmes's Holes'. These represented gateways to a series of seven worlds that nestled within each other. Sufficient sunlight was able to get through the holes to sustain a population of pallid creatures who were able to stay alive breathing the oxygen-thin air that reached the centre of the Earth.

In 1818 he offered to go himself to explore for these holes provided he was funded. A United States Senate vote was taken to see if he would receive Federal backing and the fact that 25 Senators voted in favour of this funding shows either how popular his theory had become or it was a reflection on the intelligence of 25 elected Senators

Golf at the North Pole

Edgar Allan Poe was another writer who must have been familiar with 'Symme's Hole', because in his famous story, *The Narrative of Arthur Gordon Pym,* he describes the young navigator plunging into the Earth's southern polar hole only to be greeted by a vast white figure which was probably meant to represent one of Symmes's blanched other-world inhabitants.

Edmund Halley, who described the comet that bears his name, had also suggested that the Earth is hollow and habitable, lit by luminous gases that occasionally escaped through the polar orifices and thus caused the Auroras.

The concept of a hollow world that could be entered through the Poles was also sustained in Jules Verne's nineteenth century novel, *Journey to the Centre of the Earth* in which his adventurers found the entrance to the fantasy world through a hole in an Arctic mountain, the Icclandic volcano , *Snaefellsjokull.*

Another legend held that the poles were Arcadian lands populated by peoples who were waiting to be discovered by other humanity -- perhaps a hark-back to the Greek Hyperboreans.

A more rational theory was that the North Pole was a temperate sea, and certainly that was believable as we sailed through the flat calm of the Barent's Sea. Not quite inviting enough to swim round the ship but to water-ski with a wet suit?....perhaps?

It was reasonable for people to think that there might be a source of warm water in the north especially after whaling fleets reported more and more icebergs in the Atlantic. It was theorised that some force was pushing the ice southwards and this could not be a force from the land, because otherwise ice would stick to it; there had to be a sea with currents pushing the ice south. Since the currents flowed south could it not therefore be that the sea at the North Pole was the global cistern that fed the worlds' oceans?

This theory was thus very damaging to those who believed that there had to be land at the top of the world. This doubt was used by John B Sheldon who tried to fool people that he had sailed to the Pole and had found a large pinnacle of rock. Although we will presently come to some other false claims by explorers saying that they had reached the North Pole, Sheldon's attempt was far too amateurish to get much mileage.

But how did people get there and where did they come from? I knew that we all came from present day East Africa where the people in the Rift Valley were the only ones to survive the volcanic eruption that wiped out the rest of life on earth. I knew that there was a drift northwards and I knew that every native Scot has evidence of African in his DNA, but it must have been the real 'losers' who ended up at the Arctic Circle.

Archeologists have found evidence of a nomadic civilisation in northern Alaska and Siberia dating from 8000 years ago but the present day indigenous population of Inuit can only be traced back to the first millennium AD; they almost certainly defeated the previous inhabitants, the Tuniit who were not at all warlike and had few weapons.

Their economy was based on the reindeer and the caribou-- the flesh was for eating, the antlers were for making tools and the skin was for clothing and footwear.

Before the first millennium however, the Vikings had invaded Scotland, settled Iceland and the south of Greenland, and had even discovered the entrance to Hudson Bay.

Greenland was warmer at the beginning of the last millennium and farmers settled there so successfully that their request for a Bishop was granted in 1124 after a delegation of leading farmers had sailed to Norway and presented the King with a cargo of ivory walrus tusks and a live polar bear! But ice core studies show that there was a rapid cooling of Greenland between 1380 and 1420.

Did the Inuit have folklore about the top of the world? The answer to that is probably not because they did not have our belief that the world is round. Their original beliefs were based on the religion practised by all Arctic peoples, from the Saami of northern Europe to the Inuit of Arctic Canada and Greenland-- Shamanism.

Instead of a sphere circling a blazing sun which itself is spinning through a dark universe, the shamanic world is a stable series of stacked planes. The top layer is the 'skyworld' which holds the sun, the moon, the planets and the stars, as well as spirits, clouds and winds.

The midworld is occupied by humans, animals and ghosts and beneath this lies an underworld accessible through caves and fissures in rocks the evidence for which is the finding of skeletal remains and fossils. Some add an undersea world populated by fish, sea mammals and, of course, spirits.

Everything that happens in the mid-world is due to influences from the sky and underworld, and to appease these malevolent spirits, the soul must leave the shaman to visit them; this is accomplished by self hypnosis or narcotics and as an accompaniment to self-hypnotic states, it is usually done to a drum beats.

Their traditions were passed down orally and since few have been able to learn their language, communication of beliefs, concepts and abstract ideas has been difficult. One thing that we do know is that they called that place that got the white men (Kabloona) excited, *'Tigishi'* which means 'the Big Nail' . One can understand why a large source of metal or iron must have been attractive to a people living year round in ice and snow and who had to exist with none of the advantages that have existed since the Stone Age. Without iron, all tools, hunting weapons, cooking utensils etc had to be carved out of bone from hunted animals. Just think for a moment how you would get on if you had no access to a source of iron. Since it was such a valuable commodity this is why the Inuits became so amenable to trade with the Arctic explorers who descended on their world, people who were willing to trade goods made from metal and iron.

As we will see later in this book some of the Inuits did have a source of iron which Robert Peary removed. What he took away from them was iron from a meteor-- their only source. Today it would be equivalent to stealing a country's supply of plutonium.

The belief that there must be a valuable source of iron somewhere in the north was underpinned whenever another *Kabloona* arrived wanting people to help him to go north even though it would mean tremendous suffering. Why would he undergo the suffering involved in going there? There had to be something worth getting and because the *Kabloona* were not divulging the secret it had to be something very valuable-- and what was the most valuable thing in the world? Iron. So at the North Pole there had to be a huge source of iron and that is why they called it *Tigishi* -- The Big Nail that was holding the world together.

But disappointingly we never either saw or met any Inuits-- nor even saw an igloo. And, to Mohammed's chagrin, no Eskimos either.

Chapter 8
The Arctic; Geography And Ownership

Bob, the lecturer from the Scott Polar Institute in Cambridge, gave us a talk on how the rotation of the earth decides our seasons and weather, why there is a six month night and a six month day at the polar regions and how the world rotates on its own axis not vertically but at an angle of 23 degrees. All baffling stuff to the layman but expertly explained by Bob.

For the first time in my life I was taking notice of geographical co-ordinates, mainly the north/south type. A large screen told us where we were minute by minute and from 68 degrees north at Murmansk this screen would show that number increasing minute by minute until it would show the magic 90 degrees, meaning we'd arrived at the North Pole.

I was standing in front of a reproduction of the map that Bob had used in his lecture which hung in a large glass frame in the lobby of the expedition teams' office. I'd never seen the world from this angle before and it is

Golf at the North Pole

the only way in which to understand the Arctic. The map is centred on the North Pole, a surrounding area of white representing the ice fields and on the right, the long north coast of Russia extending from Norway to Alaska, and on the left Greenland, Canada and Alaska. I think for the first time in my life I understood why earlier navigators had spent so much time trying to traverse the north-west and north-east passages.

I was joined by Anders, the Belgian doctor who had worked in the Democratic Republic of Congo. I asked him what the ordinates of the Congo were.

'It sits on the Equator and stretches from 6 degrees north to 14 degrees south. I worked in Kinshasa which is around 4 degrees south -- a long way from where we are now.'

He continued 'The climate is absolutely awful and you can understand why I spend so much time nowadays travelling in the icefields; there were days when I would have given a months' salary to have had some ice in the Congo'.

'Where's home in Belgium' I asked

'Antwerp. The weather there is probably as bad as your weather in Edinburgh'

It struck me that with my perpetual ignorance and lack of interest in co-ordinates, I had little idea of how far north I lived or even how far we were from Antwerp.

I asked Anders.

'Edinburgh is about 55 degrees north and Antwerp is 51' he explained.

I told him the story of Robert Louis Stevenson who had left Edinburgh for Tahiti because of the climate which he described as a 'meteorological purgatory' -- a phrase subscribed to by every citizen of the town. It's not that it's very cold, it's just grey-- not as grey as Murmansk (that's why I had a smidgeon of a 'feel good' factor there) -- but each day we in Edinburgh feel that the sky is lower than God meant it to be.

I was stopped mid-grumble by Anders telling me to be grateful that the Scots and Belgians did not have floods or droughts, tornados or hurricanes, or blizzards or heat waves to make life more difficult. But he then introduced me to another concept that had never crossed my mind.

He stuck a finger on the map stabbing first at Greenland, then Labrador and then the north coast of Canada.

'These places where 'people' don't actually live, are all at the same latitude as our cities. In fact life would not be possible anywhere above 50 degrees north if the earth did not move in an ellipse around the sun. Because of this elliptical motion and the tilt of the earth's axis, the northern hemisphere is closer to the sun in the winter than the summer allowing those of us who live at this latitude and above to have a reasonable winter existence'

'If this didn't happen then human habitation would not be possible in Greenland, Labrador and the north coast of Canada all of which are at similar latitudes to Edinburgh but without the advantage of the Gulf stream. Similarly life would be impossible in Sweden, Norway, Finland, most of Denmark and the Baltic States if the sun didn't warm the northern hemisphere in the winter. The corollary of course is that the southern hemisphere is closer to the sun in the summer than the winter and this is part of the reason for skin cancers to be commoner in Australia and South Africa than Europe.'

I knew that our temperate climate was due to the Gulf Stream but I hadn't previously realised the importance of our being closer to the sun in the winter.

The Gulf Stream certainly does not get round the corner of Norway to the north coast of Russia which forms ninety nine point eight per cent of the eastern coast line of the Arctic; the zero point two percent represents Norway's Arctic coast. Russia represented just about the whole of the right hand side of the map.

In the nineteenth century, when trade with the Far East was becoming increasingly important, many attempts were made to find a short-cut from Europe to the East. The main mass of sea north of Russia is the Arctic Ocean but it is so enormous that different bits have different names such as the Barents, the Kara, the Laptev, the East Siberian and finally the Chukchi Sea leading into the Bering Straits which divides Alaska from Russia.

You might wonder why there is still a need to sail along the enormous length of the north coast of Russia now that road, rail and air transport is so efficient but Siberia is such an enormous land mass that it is not all served well by communications and the sea lane must often be used. This is why Russia has more nuclear ice breakers than any other country because they're needed to guide convoys along this north coast in the winter months.

In the nineteenth century when global trade was expanding, speed and convenience became increasingly important. For example to get from Archangel in the north west of Russia to Japan, a ship could either sail along the north coast of Russia, through the Bering Straits between Alaska and Siberia and down into the Pacific and between the Aleutian and the Kuril islands to Japan -- or south, around the Cape of Good Hope and eastwards to Japan.

While sailing along the north coast of Russia might seem the shortest and most direct route, the north coast of Russia is so long that it is not a lot quicker than going west into the Atlantic, round the Cape of Good Hope and through the Indian Ocean to approach Japan from the south -- and that doesn't need ice breakers. But finding this out caused a lot of hardship and loss of life.

It was as late as 1878 that the Finnish-Swedish explorer Adolf Erik Nordenskiold made the first complete passage along the north of Russia in a ship called the *Vega*. But in retrospect while this was lauded as a 'breakthrough' at the time it didn't turn out to be all that important because in the next 30 years, of the 122 convoys that attempted the journey, only 75 succeeded in completing it, and they only managed to move as little as 55 tons of cargo.

The importance of the long Russian Arctic coastline however gives the country a big say when the subject of ownership of the Arctic region comes up for discussion.

Golf at the North Pole

There are five countries with Arctic borders -- Russia, Canada, Denmark (owners of Greenland), Norway and the United States. Surprisingly the only significant disagreement is between America and Canada. America claims that the waters to the north of Canada are International waters open to everyone-- but Canada, of course, disagrees. Even the long-standing dispute between Russia and Norway as to the maritime boundaries of the Barents sea has been settled amicably because there are ample mineral resources on each side of the border.

The relatively peaceful and relaxed discussion about 'ownership' is probably because of skillful Scandinavian leadership, but there was a slight blip in the cosy relationship in 2007 when a privately funded Russian expedition planted a Russian flag on the sea bed beneath the North Pole at 90 degrees north.

The expedition was led by Artur Chilingarov, a Russian explorer and a former member of the Duma. The party arrived near the Pole on the ice breaker *Yamal* and even though it was only six years ago, the ice was much thicker than today and it took them seven days and nights to arrive. Once at 90 degrees north, they descended in two submersibles through a hole in the ice and went down to the floor of the ocean (14,000 feet), a journey that took them 3 hours.

Chilingarov himself was in the first submersible which planted the titanium flag on the sea floor using a robotic arm, but there was nearly a tragedy when the second submersible took almost 2 terrifying hours to find the ice hole in order to surface.

No diplomatic incident occurred as a result of this venture because planting flags no longer 'counts' for claiming territory. The days of a British Naval officer arriving on a beach, planting the Union Jack and claiming the land for Queen/King and country have long since gone.

Who owns what below an ocean is governed by the International Law of the Sea. This Law entitles countries to an area of the seabed beyond the usual 200 nautical miles with certain provisos. The most important proviso is that if a country can show that their continental shelf extends further than the 200 nautical miles then that country can make their claim to the extra sea bed.

The so-called Lomonosov ridge is the part of the Arctic Ocean bed that is rich in minerals and lies under the pole; it is claimed by Russia, Canada and Denmark. When the flag was planted it was assumed that this was Russia making their claim -- but it wasn't. Although it was led by the Russian polar expert Chilingarov, it was initiated by an Australian entrepreneur and a retired American submarine commander and paid for by a Swedish pharmaceutical tycoon.

Most countries in the region have a romantic notion of their Arctic frontiers swathed in mystique and folklore but a certain reality is added by both Russia and Canada. Both these countries see the Arctic as vital for their military security.

Apart from Scandinavian chairmanship of the Arctic group of countries there are some other very important reasons for relations being so amicable. Of these perhaps the main one is the high cost of developing the resources

Golf at the North Pole

of the area and the negative aspects of a dispute which would result in delays in exploitation. In 2011 the first binding agreement was signed and that was related to the important problem of coordinating search and rescue efforts. Rival oil companies are also co-operating on scientific research and geological mapping.

Another important catalyst to co-operation is the fact that if the littoral countries agree, then there is no reason for any other countries to get involved in a part of the world where they are neither needed nor wanted. The five countries are much better off having it all to themselves rather than spending years in international courts fighting about who owns what.

The ownership of the mineral-rich Lomonosov ridge will be settled by the countries themselves because the United Nations does not adjudicate disputed territory and whatever the outcome, it matters little because there will be plenty of minerals remaining for the losers.

The next biggest 'owner' of the Arctic is Canada, and finding a way through its scattered northern coastline was once the more realistic dream of Europeans as a short cut to the East. As opposed to the north-east passage, a north-west passage made a lot of sense. Sailing from the Atlantic to the Pacific before the opening of the Panama Canal in 1914 meant travelling round the stormy Cape Horn and the journey would involve sailing down one side of South and Central America and up the other side.

If there was a navigable passage through the Canadian islands then it would be a real advantage. There are about 20 islands grouped together as Queen Elizabeth Islands, of which Ellesmere Island is the biggest. Slightly south of them is an archipelago, the main islands being Baffin, Resolute and Victoria.

It took two centuries of attempts and the loss of hundreds of lives before it was accepted that there was no navigable passage, at least for a ship of any reasonable size.

The first explorer to conquer the north-west passage was Raold Amundsen in a three year expedition between 1903 and 1906. Amundsen was unarguably the Master Explorer. He departed on a herring ship *Gjoa* with only six of a crew. With all his polar experience Amundsen knew that he had to have a boat with a shallow draught and since they were to be away for such a long time he also knew that they would have to live off the land and so the smaller the crew the better. After completing the passage and anchoring near Herschel Island, Amundsen, on his own, skied 800 kilometres to the city of Eagle in Alaska and from there sent a telegram announcing his success. This remarkable man then skied 800 kilometres back to his companions. That must have been the longest walk to post a letter in the history of mankind.

Although he had found a way through from the Atlantic to the Pacific he also showed that it was never going to be a commercial proposition. The reason he managed it was that he used a very shallow draught boat which was able to pass through many of the passages that were no more than a metre deep.

Although commercially non-viable, the north-west passage has been a great testing ground for adventurers and many have crossed it in different ways, the latest being in 2010 when the famed British explorer Bear

Grylls travelled with a team of 5 using a rigid inflatable boat.

Anders and I were still standing at the map half an hour later and we'd both had enough geography for the day.

'Do you know any stories about the search for the north-west passage' I asked him. 'For example do you know about the barrow boys?'

'Barrow boys don't explore -- they sell fruit from barrows' he said.

'Not these barrow boys'

He had probably either read *The Ancient Mariner* or some books by P G Wodehouse involving young men in a golf club being cornered by the Oldest Member and bored out their skulls by a nonsense story containing a moral, because he exhibited a certain hesitancy.

Perhaps it was the invitation to go up to the bar to sample the cocktail of the day that persauded him to suffer my stories.

Chapter 9
The Barrow Boys

At the beginning of the nineteenth century the British Navy was totally occupied in defending the British Isles from the threat posed by Napoleon Bonaparte, who, at the time, looked like taking over the whole of Europe. Great naval battles were fought at Trafalgar and the Nile but it was not until Napoleon was finally beaten by Wellington at the Battle of Waterloo in 1815 that the Navy could relax and think of other things.

When the threat of Napoleon disappeared, one of the initial problems was what to do with the huge number of ships and maritime manpower that they had built up over the previous twenty years. Suddenly they had nothing to do.

Sir John Barrow at that time was the second secretary of the Admiralty, a post he held for forty years after his initial appointment in 1804 and it was he who suggested St Helena as a final resting place for the captured Napoleon. He had become a diplomat early in his life and had had experience in China and South Africa before being appointed to the Admiralty. He developed a keen interest in the Arctic and along with Sir John Franklin and Francis Beaufort (after whom a famous ridge in Antarctica is named) he founded the Raleigh Club which developed into the Royal Geographic Society.

Golf at the North Pole

In the post- Napoleonic years he dispatched many expeditions to the Arctic because he was a passionate believer in the existence of an Open Polar Sea and one of the first expeditions he sent out was tasked with providing him with that proof.

In 1818 two Royal Navy ships were sent out to find this imagined Sea, prove that it was there and, in the spirit of the time, claim it for Britain. But they only got as far as Spitsbergen where they met bad weather and were wrecked; a warning of things to come.

The north-west passage had been talked about ever since the 15th century voyages of Martin Frobisher and John Davis. The dangers had been well demonstrated in 1619 when the Danish sea captain, Jens Munk, sailed two ships into Hudson Bay in late August. By the end of the winter he had lost 61 out of his crew of 64 seamen from exposure and scurvy and he limped home in the one remaining vessel a year later.

In 1828 Barrow sent off another expedition under an experienced Arctic explorer, Captain W E Parry. to find the polar sea. Parry was a suitable leader because he also was another enthusiastic believer in the fact that there was a sea beyond the ice.

A strategy was agreed of sailing to the ice barrier, crossing it on sledges, and then taking to the sea again for the final push. They created sledges that incorporated the dual function expected of them. They were basically sea-going skiffs with steel runners.

The plan was to sail as far north as was safe, prior to the ship being crushed by ice, and then to set off over the ice, man-hauling the sledges until they came to the sea, at which point the sledges would be launched as skiffs and they would sail to the Pole.

They could not take the ship as far north as later explorers because it was not built to withstand any ice pressure and at that time we were 100 years away from the technology of ice breakers.

The expedition man-hauled the sledges to 82 degrees 45 minutes (just short of 600 miles from the Pole) before turning back without having even found the polar sea.

But on this journey, Parry discovered the phenomenon that was to be the most formidable obstacle for every future explorer in the area -- drift.

At the same time as they were marching forwards on the ice, the floe they were on was drifting backwards and so it was as if they were marching 'up' a 'down' escalator; that is bad enough but to this you have to add the problem of not knowing in which lateral direction you are being carried -- and being powerless to do anything about it. Parry's expedition had marched north a distance of 700 miles over the ice, but this only represented a distance of 170 miles because of the drift.

Although this was probably Parry's major discovery, he also contributed enormously to polar exploration with some of his simpler findings. When Englishmen went out in the cold all they did was to pile of more woolens; he found out the hard way that this was not what to wear in the Arctic. Wool becomes wet and heavy and does not dry and carrying another set of dry woolens takes up a lot of room. Although he made this observation, it was not until explorers saw how the Inuit lived, that they discovered how to exist and survive on the ice. He also identified that supplies should be as compact as possible and there ought to be equipment that could cross ice as well as open sea with as little modification as possible.

The catalyst to Barrow's enthusiastic support for British Arctic exploration was Vitus Bering who had completed a voyage on behalf of Russia through the Straits between Alaska and Russia that now bear his name. As the boss of the Admiralty, Barrow felt that it would be an enormous affront to the great British Empire if any other nation achieved success before them, especially via the sea. His major concern was that the Russians might find the north-east passage before the British could find the north-west passage. The British were excluded from sailng in Russian waters and so were denied any attempt at 'gazumping' the Russians for the north-east passage. But on the other hand, since the north-west passage lay among the islands of the Canadian north, this was 'off-limits' to the Russians.

So the race was on to see who could get from the Atlantic to the Pacific first.

In spite of numerous failures Sir John Barrow continued to argue for 'one more push' and this was supported by the Royal Geographic Society. He wanted Captain (later Sir) John Ross to lead the expedition because his previous feats had labelled him Britain's Arctic expert. He and the crew of his ship *HMS Victory* had done amazingly well to survive the 4 years that they were marooned on the Boothia Peninsula and Somerset

Island from 1839 to 1843. Not surprisingly Ross's wife put her foot down and would not permit her husband to disappear for another long absence. She was prescient because the next expedition turned out to be a complete disaster.

The poor chap picked to lead it had also had a lot of Arctic experience. He was Sir John Franklin, who was Alfred Lord Tennyson's uncle. He had joined the Navy at 14, had fought at Trafalgar and while he carried out two explorations of the Canadian Arctic, surveying 340 square kilometres of iced land in 1819, 10 of his men died of cold, scurvy and starvation. He did another expedition between 1825 and 1827 and this time mapped another 640 square kilometres and for this he was knighted and sent to Tasmania as Governor.

By the time he was invited to look for the north-west passage he was really too old, 59, and the job should have been given to a younger man, but his experience and connections told and on 19 May 1845 he set off with two specially strengthened ships, *Terror* and *Erebus* with three years' supplies of food, a top quality crew, locomotive engines to help the ships break through the ice, a huge library and an early version of central heating.

After information came back to London that he had arrived in Baffin Bay and had sailed through the Lancaster Sound, he and his expedition 'disappeared'. Thereafter nothing was heard from them and after waiting in vain for some sort of communication for two years, the Admiralty sent out three expeditions to search for them.

Golf at the North Pole

One expedition was sent through the Bering Straits, one sailed through Lancaster Sound and another went overland up the McKenzie River in the far north of Canada just in case the expedition had abandoned ship and were on land. They found nothing; no relics, no bodies, no evidence-- the expedition had apparently vanished into thin air.

In the same week that the Light Brigade charged at the Battle of Balaclava in 1854, another rescue expedition led by John Rae found some Inuits who had memorabilia that could only have come from Franklin's expedition (his Order of Merit being one); disturbingly the Eskimos reported instances of cannibalism but this was ignored.

In 1857 Lady Franklin herself funded another expedition to search for her husband. The *Fox* under the command of Captain McLintock, an Arctic veteran, found skeletons in the uniform of stewards and also a note describing what had happened.

Evidently John Franklin had died on board the ship on 11 June 1847; the ship had been ice-bound since September 1845 and was finally crushed. By the time the survivors left the ship, 9 officers and 15 seamen had already died, an astonishing finding since, although caught in the ice, the crew were living in apparent comfort in a well insulated environment with 1000 bound copies of *Punch,* and had been doing so for the previous 32 months.

This was all the more surprising because in the early 1830s when John Ross and his crew had been forced to abandon *Victory*, they had managed to survive in the cold for 4 years before being discovered by a whaling ship. Ross returned with 19 of his 22 men.

It took another 140 years for the answer to come to light.

In 1981, an anthropologist from the University of Alberta, Owen Beattie, found the graves of three seamen, Torrington, Hartnell and Braine. The bodies of all three sailors were well- preserved because they had been buried in ground that was intensely cold and so were in excellent condition for investigation by modern methods.

Beattie compared the lead content of the bones of the seamen with Inuit bones found at the same site and discovered that the European sailors had ten times the lead levels of the Inuit.

He and his team went back to the site three years later, in 1984 and again in 1986, and exhumed the bodies, carried out radiographs, and performed autopsies before reburying the three seamen.

They found that all three suffered from tuberculosis, but that would not have been an uncommon finding in the middle of the nineteenth century, and it was not necessarily fatal in the short term.

What was significant however, and what solved the mystery of the disappearance of the whole of the Franklin expedition, was that all three had levels of lead that would have certainly led to death.

In 1845 preserving food in tins was new technology and the expedition had taken over 8000 tins with them. The contract for the tinned food had been given to Stephan Goldner in April 1845 and his firm did not have the resources to fulfill the contract in the time given them. With a couple of weeks to go, only a tenth of the contract had been completed and one must presume that thereafter quality control must have suffered.

The tins of the time were made by bending the tin sheet and soldering the overlapping faces. This meant that there would be an interface inside the tin between the solder and the preserved food and is a rational explanation of why there were so many deaths so quickly in the circumstances.

And, with the usual speed of big government, it was not until 1890 that soldering on the insides of food tins was banned!

The investigators also found signs of starvation, hypothermia, scurvy and botulism (due to contaminated food) and there was evidence that some cannibalism may have taken place. Despite the gruesome demise of Franklin and his entire body of men, the media of the day hailed him as a hero and the discoverer of the northwest passage even though he hadn't.

I was explaining why these British expeditions were absolutely disastrous, especially Franklin's but Anders was no longer listening. He was asleep. But I guess stories about the British Empire are not all that gripping if you're Belgian.

Chapter 10
Early American Explorers

The middle of the nineteenth century could have been a very boring time for a young man. We were a hundred years away from the sexual revolution of the 1960s, there were few wars and certainly nothing as exciting as an 11th century Crusade. It was time when young men were supposed to have 'feelings'; they were supposed to be artistic, creative and intellectual. Poetry would have a huge place in defining 'feelings'. But that didn't suit everyone, and so any opportunity for adventure that was advertised would be inundated with volunteers.

Two such American men in search of adventure were Elisha Kent Kane and Charles F Hall. They were both American, were both looking for adventure and they both found that Franklin's disappearance was as good an excuse as any to go exploring in the Arctic -- but with vastly different outcomes.

Golf at the North Pole

Charles Hall was 36 when he started to be interested in the Arctic. He had spent his life wandering from job to job, being apprenticed as a blacksmith and ending up as a maker of seals and engraving plates in Cincinnati, Ohio. He also published two small newspapers which must have been fairly profitable because he funded his own first Arctic expedition in 1860 when he was 39 without any outside assistance. He accomplished very little after spending a winter on Baffin Island, but wrote about his experiences in a book, *Arctic Researches and Life among the Esquimaux (*by this word he means Eskimos or Inuits*)*. The seed of Arctic enthusiasm was sown, he got his expected publicity and so he set off on another expedition in 1864. He spent time on King William Island where he mistakenly formed the impression that the Inuit who had first found Franklin's party had left them to starve to death. He wrote a lurid story about this but he was not the first newspaperman to get a lot of mileage from not allowing fiction to get in the way of the facts!

The 'Big Lie' however paid off because he was then funded to the tune of $50,000 by the United States Congress so that he could do something that had never been attempted before --- he would try to get to the North Pole.

He departed in *Polaris* with a party of twenty five in September 1871 but his power of command was flawed. The discipline of the newsroom does not translate seamlessly into a long-term bonding of males closely confined on a boat. Right from the start the crew dispersed into factions and one particularly anti-Hall faction was led by the German physician Dr Emil Bessels.

They reached their base at north Greenland and settled in for the winter. The idea of wintering in the north was to practice sledging, skiing and survival so that when spring came they could take off as masters of the ice. One day however, after returning to the boat from a practice sledging trip with an Inuit guide, Hall fell ill after drinking a cup of coffee. He recovered for a short time but then fell ill again and died, whereupon he was taken ashore and given a formal burial -- quickly.

The official diagnosis was the meaningless medical term of the time-- 'apoplexy'-- and then he was mourned by some and forgotten. But in 1968 his body was exhumed and tests showed that he had died from arsenic poisoning. The forensic examination of the diaries of the expedition resulted in strong suspicion falling on the late Dr Bessels. But by then it was too late for justice to take its course.

Elisha Kent Kane was born in the same year as Hall and was a doctor in the US Navy. He gained his Arctic experience first on a 'find Franklin' expedition of 1860-61 under the command of Edwin de Haven. This was the the expedition that discovered the site of Franklin's first winter camp.

Kane also organised and led the second Grinnell expedition which left New York in 1853 and which managed to get further north than any previous expedition, discovering the ice free Kennedy Channel which came to be used as a route to the Pole by many later expeditions.

Golf at the North Pole

Kane's expedition became ice-bound and had to abandon ship in May 1855 and even though suffering from scurvy he led an 83 day march to safety carrying the invalids and only losing one man. Kane's health never recovered from that ordeal but even though he was ailing he managed not only to write about his experience in a two volume *Arctic Explorations* but also to sail across the Atlantic to visit Lady Franklin in England in order to give her a first hand account of what her husband must have endured.

After that, with deteriorating health (possibly from TB) he went to Havanna where he died. His body was brought back to Philadelphia on a train and the journey was remarkable because at every station, the train was met by a local delegation that wanted to record their admiration for the 'Good Doctor'.

After these two expeditions the American government got serious about funding an expedition to the North Pole. In 1879, as an outcome from the International Polar Conference in Hamburg Germany, Congress charged Lieutenant Adolphus W Greely, a former Civil War cavalry officer, to set up a permanent station at Fort Conger which was at the converging northern ends of Greenland and Ellesmere Island.

Greely set up his base camp at Fort Conger and his little settlement became the most northerly inhabited place in the world.

He started with 26 members of the U S Army and the only reason we know of the horror of this expedition is that six of them survived. For two years the party explored and mapped the most northerly continental shelf in the world; at the time one of the expedition described it as "an inextricable maze of huge bergs and enormous hummocks which was impassable for any ship".

As the third winter approached the relief ship the *Proteus* did not arrive and so Greely decided that since none of them wanted a third winter in the Arctic, they would go southward on foot.

This was a disastrous decision because as they moved south through the oncoming Arctic winter they started to die one by one from starvation and disease. One man was shot on Greely's orders for stealing food and then they resorted to cannibalism as they struggled to find the *Proteus* or any other means of rescue.

Their plight became world news. Congress appropriated $33,000 for a relief ship, the survivors of another previous expedition which had almost been as disastrous, the *Jeanette,* offered their services free and many others who had been to that part of the world also volunteered to find the lost group.

A rescue party found a few survivors in a ragged tent in which Greely was on his knees, with a Bible lying on the ground in front of him. His hair was long, his eyes sunken and he had obvious scurvy. Another man lay beside him with only stumps left from his arms and legs with a spoon fastened to the stump of one arm. The six survivors were taken aboard the rescue ship but the man with no legs or arms died on the way home.

Their mapping work was of enormous importance but Greely's decision to leave Fort Conger and attempt to

Golf at the North Pole

go south as winter approached created one of the worst ever Arctic disasters .

If you are trying to cross the Arctic from East-West, you have to enter the Beaufort Sea by sailing past Alaska, which America bought from Russia for $7.6 million (today's money about $120 million) in 1867--- one of the greatest 'steals' in history. The importance of that sale however is now of increasing value because it gives America a seat at the table of littoral Arctic nations when it comes to commercial exploitation once the ice cap melts.

In the twenty first century I think it reasonable to ask 'What sort of people went on these expeditions?' They would be young men who wanted more from life than a safe job, a marriage and respectability offered. Sport in the middle of the nineteenth century was limited. Organised adventure such as going to war was not available to all and so to take part in the adventure of an expedition was a very attractive option.

Poets were writing about 'heroism'. Wordsworth, Coleridge, Shelley, Byron and Keats extolled the virtues of heroism and this concept was carried on by the Victorian poets such as Tennyson, Browning and Gerald Manley Hopkins.

The last quarter of the eighteenth century was a time of social revolution in many countries and although Britain was saved from the physical consequences of revolution, the lack of it may have frustrated young males who did not have to suffer the grind of work to make a living.

Values such as duty, resourcefulness, stubbornness, endurance and resolution were all part of upper class British life. Many of those who used the excuse of 'looking for Franklin' were thrill seekers, romantics, visionaries and withdrawers from the complications of life. They would be served by seamen who perhaps had the same sort of characteristics -- escaping criminals, misfits, malcontents, brooders and self-testers.

The original pioneers of golf would have been totally different from explorers. They would have been fun-loving men who enjoyed eating, drinking and betting and in the early days of golf were usually Freemasons because it was from Masonic Lodges that modern organised golf began. They enjoyed short-term male bonding and although there may have been many closet homosexuals it is unlikely that any openly gay activity would have been tolerated.

Chapter 11
Wild Life

Klaus, the third generation German factory owner who made bearings for both BMW and Volkswagens, had, on several occasions, seen Knut, the most famous polar bear in the world. He was looking forward to seeing the real thing in its natural habitat but seeing Knut must have been something really special because for four short years he was a world celebrity (Knut, not Klaus)

Knut was born in the Berlin Zoo in 2007, rejected by his mother at birth and brought up by keepers. His mother, Tosca, was aged 20 and had been a circus performer in the former East Germany and his father was much younger; Lars was only 13.

When Knut was born, he, together with his unnamed brother, both the size of guinea pigs, was abandoned on a rock in the bear enclosure in the zoo. They were picked up by zoo-keepers with the aid of a modified fishing net and placed in an incubator, where the unnamed brother soon died due to an infection. Knut, on the other hand, was raised by zoo-keeper Thomas Dorflein, who slept near him and fed him every two hours with a bottle of baby formula mixed with cod liver oil. After four months that was upgraded to milk porridge mixed with cat food and vitamins. He became a global sensation.

What followed was dubbed 'Knutmania'.

Sadly, the bear died unexpectedly when it was four, collapsing and drowning into his enclosure's pool suffering from encephalitis.

One of the reasons you go to the Arctic is to see polar bears. They only live between 80 and 88 degrees north and perhaps the most southerly point you'll see them is northern Manitoba.

The tour company motif was Polar bears. The little shop was full of goods emblazoned with that polar bear motif. Want a warm hat and gloves? The only ones you could get were white, made like polar bears, with eyes, heads and claws. Want a memory stick for your photos? It was there, shaped like a polar bear, with a removable head. Walk along to reception and what's on the wall posters? Polar bears.

Cuddly lovely animals? Well, not quite. They will kill you even if they are only moderately hungry and you are near them. You might keep one at bay, but you'd need a big gun because a male can grow to a height of 9 or 10 feet and weigh up to 1500 pounds.

The species are superbly adapted to the Arctic because of the huge layer of fat that surrounds their body. When you see pictures of polar bears rolling about

Golf at the North Pole

in the snow and ice they are not playing -- they're trying to cool down. Although they can run up to 25mph when chasing something, they usually amble along at only a few miles an hour in order to avoid overheating. Since seals are their main food, they spend much of their time in the water or jumping from ice floe to ice floe looking into the water. They are powerful swimmers and have been known to swim for over 100 kilometres.

As you watch one prowling about, all alone on the ice with no other living thing in sight, you wonder what on earth it is attempting to do in order to find food and survive. What it is doing is using its fantastic sense of smell by which they can smell a seal over a mile away even if it is three feet under the ice. When they discover a seal, they will dig a hole through the ice with their large claws and once the hole is made they will lie patiently at the side for hours until the seal surfaces; then it will be grabbed and eaten.

As soon as we entered the pack ice, the crew lookouts continually searched the wide expanses with telescopes and when a bear was spotted, the PA system would buzz and Laurie would announce that a polar bear had been sighted. That inevitably led to a dash for cameras and kagools. The Chinese were inevitably the first to the ship's rails, snapping away with the long lenses even though there was apparently nothing on the ice visible to the naked eye. The Captain however knew how to keep his customers happy because the ship would track the sighted bear slowly so as not to disturb it too much; each tracking might take half an hour or more.

Female polar bears mate once every three years and although this takes place around May or June the egg does not implant until the autumn. In November they find a hillside near the sea and dig a deep denning hole inside which she will dig out two further chambers. There will be two or three cubs born around January and she will stay in the den until March/April. When she emerges it is vital that she gets onto the sea ice quickly to find food because she will not have eaten for five months. Before denning she will have eaten to excess but by the time the cubs have fed off her high calorie milk for two months she will have become weak and the survival of her and her cubs will depend on her having enough strength to find food quickly. Her first priority therefore is to catch seals and if she doesn't manage this within the first few days then both she and her cubs will die. Walruses, an alternative food source, are more difficult to catch because in her weakened state she would not have the strength to kill one, nor would she have the speed to catch an arctic fox unless it was injured.

Then she will look after her cubs for up to three years before sending them out on their own.

Polar bears are amazingly agile for their size. Watching the wonderful co-ordination they show when leaping from ice floe to ice floe or coming out of the water I was left wondering why it was that I couldn't co-ordinate my arms, legs, hands, feet, trunk, neck and head so well. If I could, then surely my golf would improve.

They are enormously powerful predators and are at the top of the food chain. A male polar bear can kill a walrus even though the walrus might weigh twice as much and has foot long ivory tusks with which to defend itself. They can also kill beluga whales by attacking their breathing holes, but very seldom make any attempt to attack an adult whale of any other type.

They are sadly an extremely endangered species because at the moment there are only between 20,000 and 25,000 living in the wild and as global warming melts the ice they will have to come south, their natural habitat having been disturbed. Coming into closer contact with man may well expose them to fatal infectious diseases.

The other common mammal that we saw in great numbers was the walrus.

In 1871 Lewis Carroll wrote a poem, *The Walrus and the Carpenter,* in which he accurately portrayed their liking for oysters. He didn't get it totally accurate however - their main dietary preference is for clams, crabs and molluscs, which they don't chew but suck. They live on rocky outcrops, beaches or, further north, on ice-floes and only have two predators in nature, the polar bear and the killer whale.

Although they are larger than polar bears and fight with their massive tusks, they are slow learners and this is why, in the 19th and early 20th centuries, American and European whalers almost wiped them out because of the ease of capture and the value of blubber and ivory. Each walrus will have at least six inches of blubber beneath the skin and valuable ivory tusks that can grow as long as a metre. These tusks are used for fighting, display and rather curiously for hanging on to the ice shelf just as a climber will hang on the sheer face of a mountain using his rope and crampons. It was easy to see why they presented such easily hunted prey because they seemed quite unperturbed when we took the zodiacs alongside them as they slept. But what a smell.

Commercial walrus harvesting is now outlawed although after the mating season some hunting by Inuits is still allowed since the meat forms a big part of their diet. The whole of the animal is however used by the indigent population just as an Italian farmer will use the entirety of a pig for different items of preserved food. The Inuit use walrus hide for ropes and kayak covering, intestines and gut linings for waterproofing parkas, ivory for carving and engraving and rather eccentrically the flippers are fermented and stored as a delicacy until spring!

As the Arctic melts and the food chain is disturbed, the walrus is one animal that will have a very good chance of survival because its main food supply, shellfish from the sea bed, continues to thrive and be plentiful.

Another beautiful mammal that will certainly be endangered by global warming is the white squeaky Beluga whale, which can sound alarmingly like a canary. This species feeds off Arctic cod, which in turn feed off algae at the edge of glaciers, but as these melt and fall into the sea, so the algae and cod will disappear.

In the past the Beluga whales were almost hunted out of existence because they did not flee from hunters. Instead, with dolphin like friendliness and curiosity they would approach the whalers and be slaughtered. Fortunately they are now a protected species but as tourism in the area increases they too will become threatened by infections and pollutants. They are halfway between dolphins and smaller whales and because of this behaviour and friendliness they are also sought after by aquaria and wildlife parks.

The Chinese long lenses were out again in force as we passed the huge Rubini Rock whose vertical faces at first appear to be made of chalk but as the ship closed in on the site it became obvious that the black and white colour was due to hundreds of thousands of Brunnich's Guillemots and Kittiwakes. I was worried when the ship slowly approached the rock because of the possibility of hitting outlying rocks but we were reassured that another feature of this remarkable rock is that it goes down to a great depth almost vertically.

Rubini Rock is part of the Franz Josef Land archipelago and more specifically part of Hooker Island, which was where we went next.

A G D Maran

Chapter 12
Does Anyone Know We're Here?

Our first sight of land after leaving Russia was Franz Josef Land, an archipelago of 191 islands lying between latitudes 80 and 82 degrees north, with the most northerly island being just less than 600 miles from the North Pole. This is the nearest point of land to the Pole, other than the Canadian Ellesmere Island and the north tip of Greenland. Although it had almost certainly been discovered previously by sealers, the official discovery of the archipelago is credited to the Austro-Hungarian polar expedition of 1873, who named it in honour of the Emperor Franz Josef. Since that expedition was not officially sponsored by the Austrian government, somehow the Emperor Josef never got around to doing the paperwork that would have included this as part of his Empire. On the other hand he may well have felt that half of Europe was more than plenty for one Emperor. And, anyway, none of his friends would have wanted to visit a few snow-covered rocks.

Golf at the North Pole

So, in 1926, the Franz Josef Land archipelago was taken over by the Soviet Union since no one else seemed to want it; in the immediate post revolution years they probably wanted every bit of nearby land they could get for their own security. There has never been an indigenous population there; in fact, the only people to have lived there for any length of time are workers on Russian military, research or weather stations. Russia declared it an Area of National Security in 1937 and until the breakup of the Soviet Union no one was allowed within ten miles of the shores.

The archipelago is permanently iced-up apart from a few weeks in the summer; but when we arrived there was far more water than ice. We anchored in a bay named Calm Bay, for the obvious reason that it was an oasis of reasonable weather around which the storms seemed to pass.

The nearest land is Hooker Island, which is where the Russians established one of their many weather stations, which would have certainly doubled as early warning stations at the height of the Cold War. As a weather station, Hooker Island was as much use as the Isle of Capri because nothing ever happened in Calm Bay.

Weather stations? It's always bad weather that far north, so why did the European powers want weather stations there? It is because the weather in northern and western Europe and the Atlantic depends very much on what is going on in the Arctic. Ever since the 1920s, with international agreement, Norway, Denmark and Russia have set up weather stations on the islands north of

Russia and have given the information freely to weather centres all over Europe.

When World War 2 broke out and Germany invaded Denmark and Norway, this co-operation obviously ended. Norway formerly occupied the weather station in the Svalbard archipelago, which we didn't visit, but when Germany occupied Norway they took over the Svalbard station.

Germany had not manned any of the weather stations previously and so had no trained people to survive in the Arctic while carrying out useful observations. So in 1943 they created a special unit from the Navy to undergo training in Arctic survival, weather observation, radio signaling, astro-navigation, skiing, cooking and hunting, and they were then sent to Svalbard where the largest settlement is Spitzbergen. They were sent there for periods of up to a year, after which they were replaced by another unit.

At the end of the war in May 1945 the unit was under the Command of geologist and meteorologist Dr Wilhelm Dege. When they heard the news of the end of the war and the surrender of Germany on the radio, they carried out standing orders and burned and destroyed all their records, codes and secret instructions.

They waited. Nothing happened. They knew they would be captured eventually -- but by whom -- the British or the Russians? It was thus a wait of some concern.

One day they received a message from Tromso, Norway, asking them for their exact position. They thought this very strange because although they had destroyed all their documents they did not think the same had happened at home base. But it had. By now all their German colleagues in Tromso were in POW camps and since all their documents had been destroyed the people on the island had officially ceased to exist. They gave their position and expected to be picked up but again nothing happened and they were adjusting to the fact that they would have to spend another winter in the Arctic, all the time having no idea of what had happened to their families and homes. On the plus side however they had been very well provisioned and they had supplies for another two years. These stocks included a generous supply of schnapps.

The time passed and still no one came to fetch them but as the summer was ending, Dege and his small troop then received a radio message on September 3 1945 and they saw a small Norwegian sealer approach the station. It was the *Blaasel,* one of the oldest and most decrepit Norwegian sealers, built in 1892.

Then they saw a Norwegian in a heavy brown leather jacket row across to them from the ship.

He said 'I am Captain Ludwig Albertsen of Tromso. The Norwegian navy has ordered me to have you surrender and to bring you and your equipment to Tromso'.

Dege invited him to coffee and schnapps. Meanwhile another German and a few friends highjacked the rowing boat and had rowed out to the sealer with a crate of schnapps. There was a roaring party and the next morning no one was fit enough to load the German baggage and equipment.

Albertsen and Dege meanwhile had business to see to.

'I suppose I should surrender' Dege said.

'I'm not quite sure how one does that' Albertsen admitted.

'Don't worry, I don't either, but I suggest that as the commander of the German weather station I hand over my pistol. That will mean we have capitulated'

'OK' said Albertsen 'Can I keep the pistol?'

And they were the last German unit to surrender, 6 months after the war had ended.

Our landing site was Hooker Island, but before we were allowed off the ship we were preceded by three Russian security guards armed with Uzis and Kalashnikovs, who had been hired to stop any of us being eaten by a polar bear. Each time the drill was the same.

The ship would stop, we'd be told to get ready to go ashore, we'd wait expectantly and when the three-man squad declared it a polar-bear-free environment we were put into the zodiacs and buzzed landwards. We were beginning to wonder if all this was perhaps over the top but on this occasion it proved to be prudent. The squad had found a hole from a polar bear's den. This indicated that a polar bear had dug her way out of her den with her cubs fairly recently, and since food at that point would be a top priority with her, then it was a dangerous situation for us. The guards scoured the hillside for about an hour before we were put in our zodiacs and allowed to go ashore.

We saw our security guards positioned in an arc high up on the hillside so that we could safely paddle about in the marshy ground photographing lichens, arctic crocus and purple saxifrage that seemed to be growing in abundance.

It was the Russians who had manned the weather station on our landing site on Hooker island. The island we landed on from our zodiacs resembled a film-set of a deserted decaying western town. Nearly all of the wooden buildings were intact but the wood cladding was whitened by exposure to many winters. Walking around you saw the living quarters, the dog kennels (at one time necessary to warn of the approach of polar bears), the radio stations, the weather-research huts and the aircraft hangar which was on the beach with a slipway down to the sea. In the winter the planes would have skis and, in the summer, floats.

We saw dozens of barrels whose hoops had split and within the splayed slats we saw the stores of lime that had been used for building and repairs; ever eagle eyed for such things, Klaus brought my attention to the large sign pointing to the bar but the last drink drunk there had been more than 50 years previously.

It was a ghost settlement so well preserved that it could have been occupied there and then had the missing population reappeared. But apart from people like us no one had set foot on the island since the last weather researcher or nuclear device watcher had decamped in 1963.

The story of this weather station was not unlike that of Dr Drege and his unit. In 1941 a group of Russian researchers, soldiers and service staff were landed for an expected 7 month tour of duty. It is difficult to say whether they were lucky or unlucky, because shortly after they landed, Germany invaded Russia and came within an inch of overrunning it; millions of Russians died of starvation, disease and trauma and even more soldiers were killed in action. However those on Hooker Island were probably amongst the 100 safest Russians in the world at that time.

The only problem was that they didn't know how long they would have to stay there and what was happening in the War. In fact they had to face the possibility that they might have to spend the rest of their lives there. Unlike Dr Drege's unit who were landed with stores for two or three years, the Russians had expected to be re-supplied within a year and very soon stores ran out. Like Nansen and Johansen who we will meet shortly, they had to live off the land. The normal stretch of duty had been 14 months with half the crew changing every 7 months but at that time those who were stranded on the island remained stranded for 4 years.

That's why there was also a cemetery.

After Hooker Island we continued through the archipelago until we reached Nansen Island, so called because of the fantastic feat of survival by Fridtjof Nansen and his colleague Hjalmar Johansen, who, in 1896, survived 3 years in the Arctic and reached the unprecedented latitude of just over 86 degrees .

Here, I did not join the others looking at the flora and fauna. I headed directly for a pile of stones over which lay a large wooden beam which I knew were the remnants of one of the great feats of Arctic survival.

Chapter 13
The Norwegian Of The Millenium

In 2000, when Norway voted for the Norwegian of the Millennium, they chose Fridtjof Nansen, a man who never reached the North Pole, never played golf, but who disappeared from the face of the earth for a year and then miraculously reappeared. Before going on his Arctic explorations however he had been an internationally known neuroscientist who contributed an eponymous discovery to the lexicon of human anatomy. After his Arctic ventures he became as well known as any astronaut and he went on to become a top Norwegian diplomat and a winner of a Nobel Peace Prize. Not bad by any standards!

He was born into a well-to-do family in Oslo in 1861 and not only did he become one of the best skiers in Norway but he also excelled at the new sport of ski jumping. After he graduated in biology from Oslo University he spent some time in St Andrews, Scotland at the newly opened Marine Laboratory, (there is no record of his ever being invited to the R&A or taking part in the 'people's sport'). It is possible that during his stay in Scotland he had a preference for indoor rather than outdoor sports because he fell in love with Marion Sharp, a student from Edinburgh, and she recalls that while they were watching *Hamlet* in the Lyceum theatre in Edinburgh, he outlined for her his plans to become a '*celeb*' by being the first person in the world ever to ski across Greenland.

A measure of his personality was how he went about accomplishing this. At that time the main habitations on Greenland were on the west coast and so not surprisingly all other expeditions had started on the west because this was the 'safe' side; if you needed rescuing or needed to turn back, you were near help.

None of that for Nansen; he went from east to west so that there was no possibility of retreat. Not surprisingly, he succeeded, wrote a best selling book about the journey, *The First Crossing of Greenland* and after it was reviewed enthusiastically in *The Times* he was always referred to as *The Great Viking* whenever anything was written about him.

Perhaps in our litigious, comfort seeking, low risk lives, governed by Health and Safety regulations, it is difficult for us today to understand, but the end of the nineteenth century was a time for heroes. People wanted to take risks, to flirt with danger and if death resulted then so be it. Life was good, the Industrial Revolution had turned the world on its head, there were no wars of significance that would cause heartaches at home and literature was about heroes; Keats and Shelley had paved the way and Alfred Lord Tennyson was still churning them out. There were parts of the world that were still undiscovered and someone who wanted adventure could start with an almost blank canvas. They didn't need to have a gimmick in order to get sponsorship from a newspaper; just arriving or discovering somewhere new was enough. It didn't have to be in a hot air balloon or a bath turned into a rowing boat. They just had to be the first to get to somewhere that no one else had ever been.

At that time being the first to get to either of the Poles was a prized ambition. Every past disastrous expedition had thrown light on previously unexpected problems and the learning curve was becoming less steep. People were beginning to understand the qualities, planning and courage it needed to trek across a moving ice cap for several weeks -- and then get back!

Nansen's idea of getting to the Pole with as little risk as possible came after he had attended a lecture about an expedition known as the *Jeanette*.

This was an American expedition led by Navy Lieutenant George Washington De Long that started out in an attempt to reach the North Pole in 1879. The expedition was sponsored by a man born in Aberdeenshire, Scotland and who had immigrated to Canada when he was 25. After failing to be successful with a number of newspapers, at the age of 36 he founded a new newspaper in New York which he called *The Herald*. His name was James Gordon Bennett and he was first and foremost a newspaperman so knew the value of 'scoops'. One of his earlier triumphs had been to send one of his employees, Henry Morton Stanley, to Africa in order to find David Livingstone in 1871.

1879 was a year when the North Pole was a big story for all the newspapers and if anyone was going to be associated with it, James Gordon Bennett was determined that it would be himself. He did not however put all his cards on the table at the start because he realised that while success would sell tens of thousands of newspapers, failure would damage sales. So he planned a 'win-win' situation.

A recent failed American expedition using a ship called the *Polaris* had started a controversy as to the best maritime navigational approach to the Pole; in other words where was the best place to start from. Every previous American attempt had been made through the waters dividing Greenland from the Canadian Ellesmere Island, called the Smith Sound; but there had been so many failures with ships being crushed by ice that an alternative starting point had to be sought.

De Long persuaded Bennett that the better approach would be by going around the top of Alaska and passing through the Bering Straits between Russia and Alaska. The deal was made in which it was agreed that the *Herald* would sponsor the expedition and report on it daily with their 'on-board' reporter, William Collins.

As a starter they 'talked-up' the dangers of going through the Bering Strait to get into Russian waters and since the chance of success in turning the bend at the top of Alaska was high there would be little or no chance of failure of getting into the Arctic; that would be the first reportable success.

After that, if the ship then changed direction and made for the North Pole then there would be added excitement, more papers would be sold and any further success would be a bonus. If they didn't get there then that would just be a pity; they'd already had their success by getting into the Arctic by a novel route. So Bennett had succeeded in creating his 'win-win' situation.

The ship was the *Jeanette*.

DeLong sailed from San Francisco in July 1879 with a crew of 30 naval officers and men, and 3 civilians, one of whom was Collins, the reporter from the *Herald*. They sailed up the west coast of America but shortly after passing through the Bering Strait between Alaska and Russia, and two months after setting off, the ship became stuck in the ice.

It first drifted in the ice but when the ice started to melt it sank because the ice had caused irreparable damage to the hull even though it had been specially strengthened by steel plates.

And so on 10 June 1881 the crew abandoned ship and split into three groups. At this time they were near the coast of Siberia where it was known that along the rivers there were human settlements from where they might organise a rescue. The plan therefore was for the party to split into three groups so that each could try and find a settlement and from there try to summon rescuers for themselves and for their colleagues.

They hoped either to land on the Siberian mainland, or failing that, one of the islands making up the New Siberian archipelago. Each group took one boat; but almost immediately one sank during a storm with all on board perishing. The other two made it to the shore but then there was confusion. Without radio contact, neither group knew where the other was but in the end it didn't matter since neither found any signs of human habitation.

Golf at the North Pole

Apart from two of the stronger members, all of one group died of exposure and starvation, but the other group fared better since only 5 died. It had thus turned into one of the most disastrous polar expeditions ever, with 18 out of a crew of 33, including DeLong, dying.

The following summer searchers found their bodies on Kotelni Island, north of the New Siberia group. They found DeLong's journal and the last entry, in a barely readable scrawl, was dated 30 October 1881.

The *Jeanette* disaster however was to have an important bearing on the race for the Pole a decade later. In 1884, an Inuit hunter found piles of clothing near a village on the south west coast of Greenland. These were identified as coming from the *Jeanette,* and further investigation showed that the wreck had drifted more than 4000 miles in three years, apparently across the top of the polar cap and down the east coast of Greenland carried by an Arctic current from one side of the world to the other.

When he found out about this, Nansen realised that there was probably a constant drift in the Arctic from the Siberian coast to the Americas. To test this novel concept therefore he realised that if he could have a ship constructed that would not be crushed by the ice, the current might move the ship together with the ice floe surrounding it, to the Pole, or at least near enough for a small party to ski the rest of the way.

But the sort of ship he envisaged had not yet been designed. It would have to have such a shallow draught and be so rounded that no shipbuilder, unless ordered, would ever follow such a design because the result would be unsaleable. Such a design renders any vessel totally unstable in any sort of sea and the discomfort of the constant pitching, rolling and yawing would be unacceptable. But that wasn't the point. It wasn't meant to be a boat that gave a comfortable ride -- it was meant to be a boat that would survive the pressure of ice and that would drift.

He managed to persuade a boat builder to work with him in designing this unusual object. The marine architect was another Norwegian of Scottish descent, Colin Archer. In those days there were many places in the North of Scotland which were nearer Norway than the south of England and the populations naturally related to Norway rather than London. For a time therefore Norway became an alternative to the other outposts of the Empire for Scottish families wanting to leave the poverty of their land.

One of these families bred the famous composer Grieg.

The craft that Nansen and Archer designed was, at the time, quite revolutionary. They created a round-bottomed boat with little draught so that when the ice closed in, instead of being crushed, the ship would merely rise as the ice froze and thereafter it would stick on the ice like a cherry on a cake. It was a sturdy ship made of American elm and oak, resembling a large cockleshell. Three layers of wood gave it a thickness of two feet, and at the bow it was reinforced to four feet with iron plates. Nonetheless it became a very comfortable cockleshell once it was fitted out. Realising that it was to be home for a crew for at least three years

Golf at the North Pole

he made sure it had auxiliary motor power, triple insulation and also the new invention of electricity that would allow them electric light during the polar winter. He added a huge library with more than 1000 books and the end result was said to resemble more a gentleman's club rather than an expedition ship. It was rigged as a three masted schooner but It was certainly not a vehicle onto which anyone with the slightest degree of motion sickness should have ventured because it rolled and yawed like a bucket in any sort of a sea.

They called it the *Fram* meaning 'Forward'

Nansen had always favoured small expeditions because the fewer the travellers the fewer supplies were needed and the chances of complications were less. He advertised for 12 men, but hundreds applied from all over the world and from them he chose twelve well-trained and securely screened individuals. One who was turned down (because his mother would not let him go) was Roald Amundsen, who at the time was only 20. Another was the English 'gentleman explorer' Frederick Jackson, who was to have such a pivotal part to play in the unfolding story. Hjalmar Johansen, an Army lieutenant, expert dog driver and skier, was so determined to go, that he even accepted the lowly job of a stoker; and as Fate had it, he was to play a pivotal part in the final drama.

They left Oslo in June 1893, picked up polar clothing from the Lapps in the north of Norway and dogs from Russia. By October they had achieved their first objective of being safely stuck in the ice with an undamaged boat; and with the internal heated and lighted environment planned by Nansen and Archer, the party were very comfortable.

It was the end of the nineteenth century and 'touchy-feely' management techniques had not been invented. The model of command was based on the discipline used by Prussian Generals and British Naval Commanders. Shortly after they had left Russia there was a party on board where a lot of the crew got drunk. Nansen read the riot act and forbad the drinking of alcohol except in very special circumstances.

Once in the ice they started drifting and to their great delight found that they had covered 44 miles in the first 10 days, but thereafter, their progress slowed, and by the next March they had only succeeded in covering another one degree of latitude that represented about 70 miles which was less than half a mile per day. In attempting to find an answer to this dramatic drop in progress Nansen figured out that his theories about drift pattern did not apply when the continental shelf dipped, changing the ocean from shallow into deep water. If he had got this right it meant the end of the hoped-for drift because from this point there was only deep water between them and the North Pole He was going to have to put on his skis and walk.

He spent that next winter of 1894-95 training all the crew in skiing, dog driving, sledge technique and fitness, and most importantly in survival technique. His reason for this was not only to keep them occupied with some sort of routine and purpose, but also to see who would be the most suitable person to accompany him on what he hoped would be the final leg of the trip to the Pole.

Golf at the North Pole

When the winter ended and the sun appeared in March 1895, the time for the final leg of the journey had come; they had drifted to 84 degrees north. Nansen set off with Lieutenant 'Stoker' Hjalmar Johansen. During the initial part of the journey the crew had found Johansen a difficult man but being a former military man he responded to Nansen's old fashioned command style and was described by Nansen as "a splendid fellow both physically and mentally".

Their original plan was to ski to the Pole and then, on the return journey to arrive hopefully on one of the islands in either the Franz Josef Land or the Svalbard archipelago depending on where the drift took them. Once there, they knew that they would eventually find a sealer or whaler that would take them home to Norway.

After 14 days they found that they had only averaged 10 miles a day because of the three things that complicate any attempt to walk or ski to the North Pole.

The first are the huge rugged hummocks of ice that they had either to manhandle their heavy sledges over or take a detour around, a step which might represent an extra mile or two. Although today, our nuclear powered ice breaker showed us that the thickness of the ice was less than a metre, at the end of the nineteenth century there were reports of 6 metres of ice. When ice is that thick it drifts less but there is more pressure exerted on it by the underlying sea currents and at interfaces of pressure zones the ice rises up like the front row of a rugby scrum, sometimes to the height of a two storey building.

The next problem are the leads, or expanses of water that become evident when ice floes separate; these have to be either crossed with a boat or again by taking a detour which might be very lengthy.

Finally they were walking on drifting ice; when the ice is going in the same direction as you you make good time and distance, but if you are walking against the drift then it is like walking along a moving walkway in the wrong direction.

Of these three obstacles during their journey they found that the drift was the worst. After another week they found that they were making such slow progress that they were still 230 miles from the North Pole; if they pressed on they might get into a situation whereby the return journey could be impossible because even now they were 600 miles from the relative safety of Franz Josef Land.

Then they discovered that they had made a potentially fatal mistake. They had both forgotten to wind up their watches (no batteries at that time). At that time you needed a watch to calculate your longitude because you needed to know the time in order to do the calculations.

Remarkably, both men discovered that in the turmoil of decision-making about advancing or turning back, they had both made this simple error. Keeping a watch in good condition in those days would and should have been second nature to any explorer. If you didn't know your longitude, then it mattered little how far north or south you were if you couldn't tell how far east or west you were. Without knowing this they could keep on going south but would have no idea if they were going to end up either in the Barents Sea or the North Atlantic.

Two weeks later this danger was brought home to them. According to their dead reckoning and planning, they should have been in the middle of the Franz Josef Land archipelago but they were still on sea ice and there was no sign of land.

By then the environment was becoming more dangerous because the air was getting warmer, the ice was turning to slush and the leads were getting wider. Pushing skis through slush was back breaking, but trying to walk without skis was worse because they found that from time to time their feet went through the soft ice up to their thighs.

Fortunately, knowing that they would have to face leads, they had done some forward planning - they carried two kayaks on the sledges. They set them up parallel and fixed their skis across the stern and bows, an arrangement that created a catamaran type structure. This proved to be a life-saving construction because without it they would have eventually died, stranded on the breaking ice.

After 146 days, during which time they had skied over 600 miles, the longest ever ice crossing in the Arctic, and paddled across miles of leads in their 'catamaran', they found a strip of bare earth exposed by the ice. This was on one of the more northerly islands on Franz Josef Land called Cape Norway; however by this time the summer was waning and the winter was nearly upon them. It was obvious to them that they would not be able to reach Svalbard and would have to spend yet another winter in the Arctic -- but this time on their own with no electric light, no triple insulation and no library.

And there I was, standing on the spot where they had stood 115 years previously trying to decide what to do. The place would then have been crawling with polar bears and they did not have Russian security men standing on the hill with Uzi's and Kalashnikovs. And when I lifted a rock I had to wonder if it had been touched by Nansen or Johansen .

What was certainly touched by both of them was the large log I was looking at which they had found washed up at the water's edge. Without this they may not have survived, because by placing this on the rocks that formed the sidewalls of their 'house' they were able to construct a roof. It was the first piece of luck they'd had since their watches had stopped.

They started building their winter home by first measuring out a 10 by 6 foot space and used old walrus tusks to dig a 2-metre hole around which they placed boulders for walls. Once the walls were built around the hole, they put the log on top and stretched walrus hides over it. When it started to snow all the holes between the rocks were blocked and the walrus skin was weighed down and secure enough not to blow away. They covered the floor with polar bear skins and they were looking forwards to the privacy of each sleeping in his own sleeping bag; but that proved to be too cold, and they had to go back to sharing one sleeping bag.

It's astonishing to think, even 115 years later, that two men had spent several months together sharing a sleeping bag and were still being formal in their conversation. Up till then they had used the Norwegian 'polite' form of 'you' and it was 'Lieutenant Johansen' and 'Captain Nansen'. With enormous magnanimity it was Nansen who suggested that they drop the formality because 'now they knew each other well enough' and also there was a distinct possibility that neither would survive and a "Farewell Lieutenant Johansen" might have been a bit prudish even in those days

At one end of the 'house' they burned blubber, salvaged from animal hunting, for heat and for cooking but with no chimney the air was constantly black, with the result that the two of them became permanently blackened. During that winter they managed to shoot 11 polar bears and 4 walruses and so had more than a ton of food laid down.

When the better weather arrived in May 1896 they pulled their kayaks the short distance to the sea and set off 'south'. They were in the curious position of knowing how many miles they were from the Equator but had no idea of their position in relation to the zero meridians. What they had to avoid was becoming an Arctic Marie Celeste continually sailing on a sea that might be Atlantic or Barents and if they came across rough seas they would certainly capsize and drown They basically island hopped, stopping every now and then to stretch their limbs or to rest. When they reached one of the most southerly islands, Northbrook, Nansen set out skiing and exploring to see what advantage or opportunities this piece of land might present, or, even better, would there be anything to give him a clue as to where he was. Then there was a 'Robinson Crusoe' moment -- he heard a human voice.

This was coming from Frederick George Jackson, the rich quintessential Victorian gentleman who, after being rejected for Nansen's expedition had merely put together his own, helped by some funding from Lord Northcliffe, the newspaper magnate. The elegant well dressed Jackson approached the coal-black shaggy Nansen, somehow recognised him and, as any well brought up Victorian gentleman might say "By Jove, I'm devilish glad to see you". Photos were taken, both Johansen and Nansen had haircuts and shaves, and apart from Nansen's piles, they were both found to be fit--- and because of all the high calorie meat and blubber they had been eating, they were fatter than when they had left the *Fram*!

Meanwhile the *Fram* drifted west, crossed the 85th parallel reaching Rudolph Island in the north of the Franz Josef archipelago. By the time they were settling down for their third winter in the ice, they found that the expedition doctor had almost used up the full supply of morphine on his own addiction. The ship got free of the ice in the May, as expected, undamaged. The curious coincidence was that this was the same day as Nansen and Johansen had left their winter house .

When Nansen eventually met up with the *Fram* and its crew in Hammerfest, Norway, he was disappointed to learn that all his efforts had taken him only 19 miles closer to the Pole than the *Fram* had drifted.

In Oslo he was received by the King Haakon and Queen Maud and in 1897 started on his series of lectures around the world. '*Nansenmania*' was spreading all over the world and he began to amass a large fortune from his lectures and his best selling book, *Farthest North*, self explanatory title because that was precisely what Nansen had achieved -- he had been further north than any other living person

Becoming too old for further adventures he got involved with the political movement that had been formed in order to campaign for Norway's independence from Sweden. This was eventually accomplished and he became his country's Ambassador to London where once again he became very popular. This was not surprising because even in the pre- television days a very big man with a booming deep voice and very little in the way of a Scandinavian accent becomes not only memorable, but easily identified. In London society, he became a great favourite of King Edward VII and also found time for several romantic affairs; among his paramours were the Duchess of Sutherland and Katherine Scott, Captain Scott's widow.

When Amundsen consulted him about making a bid for the Pole, Nansen gave him the use of the *Fram* but after departing north, Amundsen changed his mind, turned south and instead of the North Pole aimed for the South Pole which he reached just ahead of Scott in December 1911. Nansen had recommended Johansen to Amundsen as a crew member, but as the trip progressed the relationship soured probably because Johansen preferred military discipline and routine, whereas Amundsen did not have that background. Johansen was a broken man when he was excluded from the party Amundsen chose to accompany him on the final push. Unfortunately, Amundsen had failed to do what Nansen had succeeded in doing -- controlling Johansen's addiction to alcohol.

There was a tragic end to this sub-plot. Johansen came home and shot himself in a seedy hotel in Oslo.

After the First World War, Nansen, like many intellectuals, had sympathies towards the aims and principles of the Russian revolution and took a great interest in the welfare of both German and Russian prisoners-of-war. He was delegated by the League of Nations to assist in the repatriation of Russian and German prisoners and he did this work so well that he was awarded a Nobel Peace Prize in 1922.

In 1925 he returned to St Andrews as Rector of the University. After he survived the traditional 'dragging' through the town he gave a brilliant Rectorial address and attended the Ball in the evening 'taking a full and active part'.

But once again the R&A was slow off the mark and did not invite him to dinner, for a round of golf or even honorary membership.

Stuffy lot sometimes!

He died of heart failure in 1930 at the age of 69.

Chapter 14
Foreign Golf

So there I was, with five days left in which to arrange a golf tournament which hopefully would be a 'first'. OK, I might not be able to arrange a tournament over a full eighteen holes but I could certainly run a tournament over one properly constructed hole under the Rules as laid down by the R&A and USGA.

Many people have struck a golf ball at 90 degrees north before. The Russians, who think they own the Arctic, each year set up a base camp fifty miles away where rich people can stay overnight and then fly into the North Pole by helicopter and do almost any activity they want. There are those who want to walk round the world, swim under the ice, run in an organised marathon or para glide onto the ice. Many are also given a club and an orange ball and might say that they've played golf at the North Pole but there has never been an actual golf tournament where men and women play against each other. In order to achieve this I would have to design a hole that, like all good golf holes, would present the player with options depending on the weather conditions, and would make the choice of shot a risk or reward experience; and there had to be dignity, atmosphere and above all, tension. All of these factors are essential for the playing of any golf hole and the spirit of this has been enshrined over the decades by the beautiful prose of great golf writers such as Bernard Darwin, Henry Longhurst and Peter Alliss.

The obvious problem for me however was that there were only two other regular golfers on board -- Don and Shirley from South Carolina. They were, like myself, golf course collectors and had obviously played all over the world and so that was the pair that I needed to lock into the project; I thus targeted them by sitting at their table whenever the opportunity arose.

As we talked about strange courses that we'd played, Don drew first blood by telling me that he'd played at what he thought was the most northerly golf course in the world which is in Ulukhaktok in Canada's Northwest Territories. Billy Joss was a Scot (who else would start a golf club?) who arrived in Canada as a Hudson Bay Company trader. He built his course on the tundra off the Amundsen Gulf in the Beaufort Sea at latitude 70 degrees 44 minutes north. He died in 1980 and in his memory the members run his Memorial tournament every Solstice. It is played over a nine-hole course and although the average temperature is below zero most months of the year, it rises to an astronomical 13 degrees above in July when golf is possible 24 hours a day.

I spent a few dollars to phone St Andrews for verification of this because in the to-ing and fro-ing for golfing supremacy between Don and myself he was certainly leading by one set to love with his first thrust. Much to my chagrin it turned out that he was right-- he had played on the most northerly golf course in the world; but it was only a nine hole course. According to the R&A ,the most northerly 18 holes course is the Tromso Golf Park at Breivikeidet, near Tromso, Norway and this lies just south of Ulukhaktok at 69 degrees 48 minutes north.

Recovering from this set-back, and at least being able to (apparently) take it in good heart, I was about to try and parry this first thrust with one of my northern golf stories but as I was just starting, Don said: "Oh excuse me, I forgot to say I've also played the most southerly golf course in the world at Ushuaia. We did the same as we did here on our Antarctic trip and arrived in Chile a day before the boat sailed so that we could play the course".

Things were looking bad for me in the golf course boasting contest that seemed to have developed, but I threw in my two northern golf sorties which didn't quite score heavily but it let me at least get a toehold in the game.

In 1988, at the invitation of an Icelandic surgeon who was a frequent visitor to Scotland, I went to play in the third Arctic Open Golf Tournament which was held (and is still held) at Akureyri in North Iceland over a course that measures between 4500 and 5700 metres depending on the tees used and has a par of 71. The peculiar feature of this tournament is the starting times, which are up to and including midnight. At the summer solstice in Iceland the sun never sets and so it is possible to play throughout what is generally reckoned 'night'. The format was fourball Stableford which generally means a five hour round, but at that time, in that place, time hardly matters.

My memory of that round was not associated with either my golf or my score but with a telephone call I received one afternoon later that year. I had been describing to my Icelandic colleagues an operation I performed for cancers of the upper oesophagus which involved removing the whole gullet and pulling the stomach up through the chest to form a new swallowing tube.

Icelanders are brought up reading the Sagas which tell of the deeds and daring of Nordic heroes and so on the basis of a description of the operation over a beer at a golf club, my colleagues had set off heroically to do this operation -- but had forgotten what to do if the stomach got stuck as it was being pulled through the chest. So they telephoned Scotland to find out what I'd omitted in my description of the operation. We had a telephone consultation which was transmitted to the operating surgeon who was next door in theatre and he, in golfing terms, thereafter got down with a chip and a putt!.

Just as Don had gazumped me with his Ushuaia follow-up story I responded with my experience of playing the Tornio Golf club at Levi in Lapland, which is unique in having the first nine holes in Finland and the second nine in the town of Haparanda in Sweden; but happily the towns are twinned and the IKEA store in Haparanda has notices in Swedish and Finnish and takes both currencies.

Don and Shirley had played most of the main courses in America apart from Augusta where only 'the elect' are allowed, and like me they baulked at playing courses such as Pebble Beach that asked for a green fee only available to a Republican. We talked of the Kiawah Island course in South Carolina where the USA had beaten Europe 14-13 in 1991 with Bernhard Langer missing a short putt on the 17th to finish the game. Don and Shirley had evidently played it well but I told them of one of my great humiliations which climaxed when my fifth shot from the tee failed to reach the island that is the seventeenth green. I turned to my partner, a particularly famous American surgeon, and said

"George, isn't self loathing a symptom of clinical depression?". And the reply was,

"No Arnie, not when it's appropriate".

I have never played well away from home. My excuses are, in the following order-- borrowed clubs, unfamiliarity with the course, talking with my host and usually a degree of jet lag. The problem is my membership of the R&A. Even though it was 'accidental', being a member of such a club does lead partners to believe that I should have an immaculately timed poetic swing, the ability to take turf just after hitting the ball and to be able to hit at least 250 yards off the tee with barely a trace of spin on the ball so that it neither hooks nor slices more than a few degrees. Never even being able to do these things with my own clubs, on my own courses after a good nights' sleep, and never to the best of my knowledge ever having taken turf after impact, I usually spent the day making excuses explaining away my abysmal play.

Another useful excuse was of course musculo-skeletal injury -- a sore shoulder, a pulled muscle, a sprained wrist or some other convenient untruth. I certainly had to remember to pull back in obvious pain when I played my commonest shot which is one which directs the ball past cover point's left hand (a shank). After one of these I would grasp an elbow or a wrist in *faux* agony to provide an excuse.

Another particularly humiliating round occurred when I was celebrating surviving the first fifty years of my life when I went to the Isle of Man for perhaps the worst round I've ever played and the only time I've failed to get into double figures in a Stableford.

The Course was the famous Castletown, and on the previous day, I had fulfilled another ambition by hiring a motor bike and driving the TT course in Douglas which still had the protective bales set out on the dangerous corners-- admittedly a hundred yards ahead of any point that I would have hit had I fallen off. Even though my motorcycle riding was slightly better than my golf, my time was more than three times that of the averages set the week before.

But back to Castletown; among the many books I'd collected over the years about famous golf courses, Casteltown featured in all of them and so I was really looking forward to the round. Another reason that was going to make the round special was that I was meeting up again with a very old and dear friend, who had made enough money as a London surgeon to retire to the Isle of Man in his mid fifties, and who was hosting me. He, like myself, was a poor golfer, so the day beckoned as a stress free round with no need for excuses; that lasted about six holes because by then, the only one of my shots that had lifted off the ground was a putt. In front of nearly every ground shot was a whin bush of impenetrable thickness and with gathering embarrassment I gave up even attempting to find balls and entered a 'blob' on my scorecard-- but it was 'blob' after 'blob'. Shamefacedly I handed in my card and found that I'd narrowly missed the wooden spoon which had gone to a man who had not played golf for twenty years and had only come along to make up the numbers.

My excuse of post traumatic stress after the death-defying 60mph ride around the TT course carried neither weight nor conviction.

Both Don and I had played all the main courses in Australia but by rather different routes. Don was a Vietnam War veteran and had taken his rest and recreation breaks in Australia and had played from Brisbane to Perth. Again he had had a wonderful time and enjoyed his golf, never having to employ the duplicity which was essential to my 'away' games.

It was different in my case. In 1993 it was with a great deal of trepidation that I signed up for an R&A trip to Australia. I was in the middle of another period of shanking but I'd bought the new (and at that time) huge, Yonex driver together with their 3,5 and 7 woods which, with a 7 iron to hit the ball along the ground for approach shots, was as near to a shank free set of golf clubs that I'd been able to put together. The tour had been arranged to celebrate the Centenary of the Royal Sydney Golf Club and during the trip we were to play matches against all the Australian 'Royal' Clubs.

On the outward journey we had stopped off at Singapore where I'd previously played all the courses and so I feigned illness hoping that if I treated the shank as an infectious disease, time would go some way to healing it. Instead of playing golf I visited some old friends in the Singapore General Hospital and tried to keep my mind off the travails that were to follow. They say that a 'shank' is all in the head, but my hands, legs and pivot also play a big part.

Our first destination in Australia was Perth, the beautiful City on the Swan River. An immensely rich R&A member took us sailing on the Swan River on his yacht and since in 1993 the evils of alcohol had not yet penetrated the Public Health debate, we all came off 'pie eyed'. We gave Royal Perth a miss because all the 'golfers who matter' in that part of the world were members of Lake Karrinyup where the fairways are populated by kangaroos with their little 'joeys' in their pouches. Being used to betting on the usual ouzles, twozles, ferrets, sandy ferrets etc I was here introduced to another side bet -- the Fairy. That represented a bet that was payable to those whose drives ended up on the fairway by those whose balls went into the rough or a hazard. All you have to do coming from the nether-reaches of golfing ability is to budget. Realise that every game of golf is going to cost '£x', be glad if that's all it costs and pay up.

Adelaide, the next city in which we were due to play, was a bit of a lost couple of days. The organisers had arranged for a tour of three wineries in South Australia. We got to number one, had lunch, tasted a lot of wine and since everyone went into a deep sleep when they got back on the bus, they took us back to the hotel so as not to disturb us --- after of course apologising to the other two wineries for our 'no-show'. The side effects of that

Golf at the North Pole

lunch were used as my excuse the next day and of course it was received both with sympathy and understanding.

Melbourne and Brisbane passed uneventfully and pleasantly but the party at Royal Sydney was purely hepatotoxic due to their marvellous wine cellar. The golf the next day was, as usual, just awful, but everyone had a good excuse. I had managed to conquer my shank during that memorable three week trip by taking a stiff arm swing that went fore and aft in as straight a line as I could manage. I didn't hit it far, but I hit it often.

By this time I could tell that Don was getting bored/tired/drunk. Much of this conversation had taken place in the bar over vodka cocktails. I suggested we call it a day but Don said "I'm more interested in St Andrews golf than stupid courses. Tell me about the railway sheds on, is it the 17th, the famous road hole?"

"Well the railway's now gone but the Old Course Hotel that bought the ground from the Railway Company rebuilt sheds so that the profile of the old sheds still faces you as you stand on the 17th tee."

But by now, with the vodka talking, I was in full flight and told him what I thought was the best 'railway at St Andrews' story.

When the 1950 British Amateur Championship took place in St Andrews, the town held its breath for the arrival of one of the biggest film stars of the time, Bing Crosby, who then played off a handicap of 2. Huge crowds turned out to watch him practice and the crowd that followed his first round match against a local joiner, Jimmy Wilson, required marshaling. After starting birdie, birdie, par, to be three up, Bing's game fell apart and he was beaten on the 16th green.

As a result of that visit, Harry Crosby (Bing) and Jimmy stayed in touch, and a year after another visit to the course in 1971, Bing was persuaded to present a trophy to be played for annually by the senior members of the R&A, the New Golf Club and the St Andrews Golf Club. In 1995 it was won by Sean Connery.

A few years later, Jimmy was playing in the final of a St Andrews Golf Club trophy over the old Eden course, when on the old 10th, beside the railway line which at that time was still in operation, one of the threesome collapsed. Fortunately a train was progressing slowly down the line on its way into St Andrews from Leuchars Junction. Bob hopped over the fence and stood in the middle of the line waving the train down which fortunately, at the speed it was going, was possible. The collapsed golfer was carefully lifted into the guard's van (necessary on every train in those days) and the train resumed its journey into St Andrews. Jimmy and his partner sorted out the cards, and carried on playing; on their return to the club to hand in their cards they were shocked to be told that their erstwhile partner was dead. After getting over the shock Jimmy wryly remarked that it could have been worse had the train not stopped "It could hae been me as well and then there wid hae been twa o' us deid".

While I was telling this story, we had another vodka cocktail and Don fell asleep at the bar while I went back to the cabin as quietly as I could so as not to wake

Mohammed who would have to get up in an hour or two for the first prayer of the day.

Chapter 15
More Foreign Golf

I was woken in the morning by Mohammed coming back into the cabin having played badminton with the crew on the night shift. He'd prayed at 4am, moved quietly out of the cabin and as he appeared again, Laurie's voice was coming across the PA system giving the outside temperature, wind speed, sea and ice conditions and what we would learn after breakfast.

None of this was of very much interest to me at that time since I was suffering from an overdose of vodka (and whatever Wolfgang had decided was last night's recipe). Mohammed quickly diagnosed my medical condition even though there were no outward clinical signs and he started to talk about the evils of alcohol and the wisdom of the Koran in banning it.

I related to him the large number of high-ranking Moslems whom I had met in the past who seemed able to drink expensive whisky quite openly and copiously.

Golf at the North Pole

'Openly?' queried Mohammed 'I doubt it'

I had to agree. Most of the alcohol movement I had been a part of in Arabia was inside the beautiful gated palaces in which the top brass lived.

'Why is alcohol forbidden' I asked him. 'I can understand how almost everything in Islam developed when the Prophet was leading a nomadic tribe through the desert but why alcohol, which in those days would only have been low alcohol wine?'

He said 'If a substance intoxicates in large doses then it is also forbidden in small doses so much so that I will not eat anything that has even been cooked in alcohol'

I raised my eyebrows and again asked 'Why?'.

'Intoxicants take your mind off God and prayer'.

I felt that ended this particular conversation and wandered off for breakfast and another five rounds with Don about experience on 'away' golf courses. Mohammed was however correct in his diagnosis and mild rebuke. My mind was more involved with my headache than any desire to pray.

On the upper deck there was a large coffee lounge and library where our position was displayed continuously on a screen and as if to keep it company, under that screen sat a group of 6-8 Chinese computer shop owners who played Texas Hold'em round the clock. Sure enough when Don and I arrived to further discuss golf they were hard at it.

This morning I brought up the subject of caddies, a word that goes back to the time that the French-educated

Mary, Queen of Scots, stayed in St Andrews and had a young 'cadet' carry her clubs.

Since, in those times there were no golf bags, clubs had to be carried much as a bunch of garden canes might be, either in one, or more commonly, two hands. Over the years it has become a good way of earning a few bob if you have nothing else to do on the Old Course at St Andrews; 'a few bob' more often than not comes out at £50. All, or almost all, St Andrews caddies are local and since no one brought up in Scotland has ever had any reason to be a racist, the attitudes once displayed by the Augusta Golf Club towards people's skin colour jarred golfers world-wide. Clifford Roberts, the chairman of the club was once reported to have said something along the lines of 'white men play golf and black men carry clubs'. I have never therefore been comfortable with another human being carrying my clubs but if my attitude was endemic around the world it would be damaging to many local economies.

I recall one particular occasion when I played Lilongwe golf course in Malawi, one of the few times I've beaten my host, (on this occasion a Malawi gynaecologist). I was allotted a caddy called Rafael who had been brought up in a Catholic mission. Malawi is one of the poorest countries in Africa and to get to carry a Brit's clubs looked like being Christmas for Rafael. He was a very polite boy, did his job well although he knew nothing about golf or the course, and started begging for a tip around the fifteenth. My heart softened and I gave him what I would have given a caddy at St Andrews had I taken one. He looked at the money wide-eyed and said "Doctor, I'll be able to buy mealie for my family for a year with this". This generosity was soon regretted when shoals of letters started arriving in Scotland begging me to set him up with a chicken farm.

He wasn't that good!

The most caddies I've ever played with was in Yangon Golf Club in Burma. There it is usual for each golfer to have a caddie to carry clubs, a tee caddie (to put the ball on the tee and to prefer the lie on the fairways as allowed by local rules), a forecaddy to spot the ball and to find the wayward shot, and one who at first seemed to have no very specific job but her use became apparent as I started to walk up the first hill; to my surprise I felt two small hands in the small of my back as she pushed me up the hill. That meant that there were three golfers and twelve caddies. I've never even seen that in St Andrews where from the window of the Big Room you can see every possible combination of golfers, friends and caddies. If politically you are to the right of centre you might consider it a pleasure and a privilege to have such attention, but the average European Social Democrat might have preferred to just hand out some money early on and get on with the game as they would do at home.

Don was slow entering the conversation this morning and at breakfast he was particularly quiet, but as the large amount of caffeine he'd consumed began to kick in, he began picking up the threads of where we had left off the previous evening.

I don't think he was paying attention while I was laying forth about the evil Clifford Roberts but as he recovered he changed the subject to golf in South-east Asia.

He said "When I played courses in Malaysia and Singapore it seemed that for twenty or thirty years the only names on the Champions Board in the clubhouse either started with *Mac*. -- *Macdonald, Macpherson* -- or were obviously Scottish -- *Mathieson, Murray, Campbell etc.*

Having been educated during the 1940s I had memories of world maps being coloured red from edge to edge and I was often sad that we'd let America go, but as I got older and watched the amount of red shrink I was able to look at the old Empire in a different light. The rulers of the Empire were English but middle management was supplied by Scots all of whom would have been well-educated but not wealthy. In those days, Scottish education was streets ahead of that supplied by the majority of schools in the south because education was the way out of the basically poor environment and there were huge opportunities available in India and the Far East. Since every young Scots boy would be able to play golf they would naturally congregate wherever there was a golf course-- and of course a bar.

As a fast-recovering Don told me about the many rounds he'd played in Thailand, Indonesia and Malaysia my own memory was stirred by the time I took a side trip from a lecture tour based in Bangkok to go to the northwards. After I had played a round on the course at Chang Mai I took the opportunity to go on a photographic safari to the hill tribes on the borders of Thailand, Laos and Cambodia -- the 'Golden Triangle'.

I hired a car and a driver telling him quite clearly why I wanted to go, but to him, 'taking photos' was obviously a euphemism for buying drugs. After visits to a couple of villages where several little old ladies stuck odd looking vegetable matter under my nose, it was soon obvious that my driver was clearly undergoing a new experience -- the photography story was actually true and not only was he losing face, he was losing his usual commission. As we drove back to Chang Mai, in silence, and at about twice the speed of the outward journey, my thoughts turned to the possibility of failing to make my tee time next morning due to lying shot dead in a paddy field.

Another golfing safari, which looked very ugly for a time, was when I lost the rather ancient clubs loaned to me by the Governor of Baluchistan. I had travelled to Quetta in the north of Pakistan, with two other colleagues to run a course in surgery for Pakistani doctors. We had travelled with our wives and as soon as we stopped outside our hotel we knew that we had accepted the wrong invitation.

Opposite the hotel, men were using the gutter for ablutions, the hotel rooms were almost bare and full of flies, what remained of paint was flaking and as we deposited our luggage in the reception area a rat scuttled across the lobby floor.

Rather stunned with the thought of the upcoming experience we went out with our wives to look at the place. The sight of 3 scantily clad white women damaged the rather good business being done by a man with a tame dancing bear. The bear stood no chance against three white women showing flesh. Extricating ourselves from the crowd and no doubt because of the language barrier missing several monetary offers for our wives, we demanded that the women be taken back to the Marriot hotel in Islamabad.

Realising the culture shock that we had suffered, our now apologetic hosts asked if we would like to go up the Khyber Pass into Afghanistan where the Mujahadeen had just seen off the Russians. The local economy of the tribes around that area at that time was based on kidnap for ransom and the Pakistani government even had an agent who did all the ransom negotiations in order to keep both the murder rate and the ensuing publicity down. Because of this the Governor arranged for us to travel 'up the Khyber' in an Army truck with an armed guard. On arriving in Afghanistan we walked around a pavement bazaar from which we could have bought anything from a Colt 45 to a ground-to-air missile, Uzi's, Kalashnikovs and grenades. I settled for a blood stained furry Russian hat.

When we came back (without having been kidnapped) the Governor arranged for us to play nine holes of golf at a rarely used course in the hills. It was basically nine flags in nine holes on a flattish piece of ground and between tee and green it was scrubland. The Governor gave us his clubs to share; they and the oversize ancient leather bag obviously dated from the fifties and since balls were more valuable than people in Baluchistan we had a squad of caddies who divided themselves up in to bearers, spotters and finders, the latter frequently having to plunge into muddy pools to retrieve the valuable objects.

We were taken back to our hotel in the minibus, spent three days teaching surgery and at the farewell party given at the Governor's house he asked where we had put his golf clubs. Obviously leaving them on the minibus was not the thing we should have done and from then on the official farewell became frosty and our arrival at the Islamabad Marriot Hotel was a relief.

The Scots and English seem to have a genetic need to play sport. One of the first things the BP oil engineers did when they started pulling oil out of the desert wilderness that was Kuwait in the 1930s was to build a golf course at Achmadi, their base, which is just outside what is now Kuwait City. The desert sand is compacted with oil, the bits at the side are left untouched and so the 'rough' is soft sand (on which you can ground your club unlike a normal bunker) and the 'greens' are 'browns' (sand heavily oiled) which are kept smooth by an Egyptian or a Yemeni (the equivalent of black caddies in the old days at Augusta) who will pop up from their dugouts as soon as you've left the green with a long thin whisk with which he expertly sweeps over the footmarks, so that it is in pristine condition for the next game. You play off mats and I noted a very odd local rule on the basket from where we took our mats. It read 'Golfers must not place their ball on the end of the mat so that it is teed up'.

Those early pioneers had also built a clubhouse and a bar but the country is officially dry and the only place you can get proper alcohol is in a home or if you are a guest of a government official.

From the Middle East the talk moved back to India where Don had once been stationed when he was in the Military. The US Navy had a base in Bombay and they had constructed their own 9 hole course. We found that we had also both played at the prestigious Willingdon Club in Bombay where I had the pleasure of playing with the Nawab of Pataudi, Mansoor Ali Khan, who joined me on the first tee for a very early morning round. He was formerly the captain of the Indian cricket team and like many cricketers, Mr Edward Dexter being the prime example, he could hit the ball a country mile with excellent timing; soft hands around the greens also made the difference in our scores embarrassingly large. Whenever I've told people that I had played with the Nawab of Pataudi I've had a reaction, but in spite of his un-American cosmopolitan life, Don still did not rate cricket or its players as worthy of comment.

Nor did he know what a Calcutta Cup was.

In 1873 a group of Empire builders formed the Calcutta Football Club and in spite of the climate, rugby was played for a number of years, membership presumably being enhanced by access to a free bar. After four or five years however the free bar could no longer be afforded and membership dropped off. The remaining members took the Club funds out of the bank in the form of silver rupees and had the three Calcutta cups created. One is for polo, one is for the foursomes championship of the R&A, but the most famous is for the winner of the Scotland-England rugby match. Don didn't *do* rugby either.

One of my trips to India was particularly memorable because I met Mother Teresa. I was shown her hospice and the orphanage and her small lecture to me as I left was withering. She said:

Golf at the North Pole

"You are very lucky being a doctor, but you must remember that Medicine is not a profession, Medicine is not a business-- Medicine is a vocation!"

That was basically true in the greater scheme of things but it wasn't what a typical western surgeon wanted to hear. It was probably thinking about this that made me forget my usual dietary care in India.

I must have eaten salad or drunk some unclean water, because as I was lecturing the next morning, I could hardly concentrate on my presentation because I knew I was about to throw up at any moment. Fortunately I managed to finish the presentation without embarrassment either to myself or to the audience of young surgeons, but golf was quite out of the question; all I wanted to do was to lie down and either be sick or die, it mattered little which came first.

One of my great friends, the late Keith McKenzie, who was the Secretary of the R&A from 1968 to 1987, was a pillar of the Royal Calcutta Golf Club in the immediate post war years, and I had promised myself that one day I would play there. This was the time-- but I was sick!

My hosts had arranged for one of the best local medical golfers, a thoracic surgeon, to take me on to Royal Calcutta. The young trainee who had been designated to drive me to the Club encouraged me to travel with him if only to see the course that I'd come such a long way to play and more importantly there was no means of contacting the thoracic surgeon.

By the time we arrived at the club, a monument to very faded elegance, I was feeling a little better, with some will to live, but none at all to play golf. The thoracic surgeon was disappointed and took me one step further.

He said " The first and last holes are parallel. We can play the first and turn round and play back so you can tell your friend that you at least played part of his course".

Reluctantly I agreed.

The first hole is a 400 yard par 4 and flat with an undefended green. Feeling as weak as I've ever felt, I hit a 210 yard drive followed by a perfect three wood to within 10 feet of the pin; I holed the putt. Summoning up my remaining strength I whispered to my host that perhaps we could try 'just one more on the way out'. That too turned out well and after the first nine I was only three over par -- perhaps my best golf ever.

I felt the weakness gradually dissipate, and as it did, my swing got faster and the ball resumed it's usual behaviour when hit by myself. My 45 for the back nine (with a few 'given' long putts) saw normal service resumed.

When I returned to the changing room I had a shower and I was astonished to find the 'drying wallah' standing outside the shower. He was holding the biggest fluffy towel I had ever seen and he engulfed me in it. I thought that that was pretty good service and set about using it to dry myself but the 'drying wallah' was having none of it. His job was to dry the sahibs and nothing was going to stop him drying me -- all over.

Perhaps I was his only customer that day or perhaps he was a pervert, becauset he certainly insisted on completing the job!

At this point Don, who was taking less and less interest in my monologue, made his excuses and went back to his cabin, leaving me wondering whether he was still suffering the side effects of the night before or whether I had taken on the mantle of a P G Wodehouse 'Golf Bore'.

3000

Chapter 16

Hot Air Balloons

It was several days before I had identified all of the expedition crew and found out what they were supposed to do. Ted from the mid-west was unquestionably the doctor, the other Bill from Canada, together with Andrew, Burt and Roger were 'logistics', Norm, Bob and Milo were the lecturers, Norma worked in the shop selling polar bear 'things' and Laurie was the leader. We of course very quickly became familiar with the two barmen, Stefan and Wolfgang but there were two other guys whose roles had still escaped me.

There was a little Russian chap who appeared after the initial introductions. He was called Alexei, and it turned out that he was the helicopter pilot. I knew that helicopters were far too far away to take any geriatric invalid to safety but as part of our package we were offered a couple of helicopter flights around the ship so we could get better photo opportunities. Helicopters have never been my favourite mode of transport so for

Golf at the North Pole

me it wasn't so much of a thrill but more of a threat to my already fast shortening life.

The other chap was large and Canadian and called Dan. He was the balloon pilot. I'd forgotten that there had also been the opportunity to sign up for a hot air balloon flight over the ice cap but since a good friend had been in a balloon that had come down in the Egyptian desert breaking his arms and legs and ruining his golf, I had scored this experience off the 'bucket list'. But many of the passengers had paid extra to have this experience. It was one of the less exciting ventures however because it was a tied balloon meaning that it was still attached to the ground as it rose to about 100 feet-- and then it came back to earth. Big deal! Big cost!

Although the flight looked unexciting Dan was interesting. As a balloon pilot (not a common occupation) he knew a bit about balloons and ballooners. I shared my doubts about this means of transport with him but he was far more enthusiastic-- as he would be, wouldn't he.

I told him about the most famous balloonist to land in St Andrews. He was the dashing young Italian Vincenzo Lombardi, who in October 1780 flew across the river Forth to land on the first fairway of the Old Course and had the Guinness Book of Records been available then, he would certainly have had an entry. Unlike Nansen, the Norwegian of the Millennium, who became Rector of St Andrews University but was ignored by the R&A, young Vincenzo was immediately made an honorary member and was introduced to golf. He played the first hole and got down in 21 shots and as far as we know he never played again having set that record. Being Italian however his priorities did not parallel those of the golfing Scottish squirearchy. A Ball was held in his honour the next evening and he recorded in his diary that "I found upwards of 100 beautiful ladies already assembled"

I asked Dan if balloons had ever been used by explorers and he then told me the story of Andre Salomon --- which did nothing to enthuse me about ballooning over the Arctic.

Present day explorers are like present day golf professionals. Every 'i' is dotted and every 't' is crossed. No detail is left to chance. Everything is checked and double checked and most modern expeditions achieve what they set out to achieve. But the importance of meticulous preparation, and its correlation with survival took a hundred years to be fully appreciated; of course advances in technology have provided more scope for choice in preparation but even so, every percentage point of detail adds to the chances of success.

But we cannot dismiss the men who did apparently stupid things because they had no experience or precedence on which to draw, and it was they who laid down the principles of Arctic survival that have made for present-day success.

In any book of heroic failures however, the attempt by the Swedish engineer Salomon August Andree must rank very high on the 'crazy' list. He used an untried technology, did the minimum of preparation and gave almost no thought as to what he would do should things go wrong. He used a hydrogen-filled balloon and hoped

Golf at the North Pole

to steer it to the North Pole by dragging ropes over the ground!

He had become an early enthusiast for the new sport of ballooning and, as a complete novice, bought a balloon in 1893, called it the *Svea* and made nine journeys in it, travelling a total of just short of 1000 miles. Several of these pioneering journeys were from either Gothenburg or Stockholm, where the prevailing wind is from the west. On one occasion he was blown right across the Baltic Sea and ended up in Finland but did not realise that he had overflown Sweden. On another trip he was attempting to balloon over the entire breadth of Sweden from west to east starting at Gothenburg, when he was again blown over the Baltic Sea, passed a lighthouse and saw breakers on a stormy sea and was rushing towards Estonia--- but he was still convinced he was still over Swedish soil and was seeing lakes!

In golfing terms, Andre was still playing off an 18 handicap when he started to play with the 'big boys'.

Unabashed by his obvious lack of expertise, he set up an expedition to fly from Svalbard right across the Arctic Ocean and land around the Bering Strait, ending up in either Russia, Alaska or Canada -- and, with luck, passing directly over the North Pole. It was in aeronautical terms the golfing equivalent of attempting to hit a 4-iron 200 yards into a left to right wind hoping to get it 3 feet from the pin!

This mad-cap idea had the expected tragic end but it has inspired several books and one film, all of which accented different aspects of Salomon Andree's daring.

Modern hot air balloons, such as the one Dan piloted, can be controlled, provided the wind is not too strong, but the type of hydrogen balloon that Andree used is at the mercy of the wind unless it can be kept reasonably close to the ground; this is why he got the idea of steering it with trailing ropes the weight of which would keep the balloon low.

The ropes were attached by screws to the basket, and if sufficient length was allowed to drag along the ground then the balloon would be slowed down so that it travelled slower than the wind. If this mechanism failed they would be totally out of control.

At first sight even to a non-ballooner this seems a dotty idea but because Andree was just about the only person in Sweden who professed any knowledge about ballooning, he had very few critics and no independent sources of counsel or advice; contemporary critics from Germany and France, who had much more knowledge of the new technology, expressed grave doubts about the safety of the techniques he proposed to use. In short, even then, a lot of people thought he was nuts.

In trials, the ropes would often become entangled or get caught in some object on the ground; when this happened the basket would be pulled dangerously close to the ground. If however either the ropes or their connections snapped off the basket, the balloon would be totally out of control and at the mercy of the prevailing winds. But he wasn't put off by any of these possible set-backs, an emotional response which could be interpreted as either courage or flawed judgement. He remained convinced that he could safely steer the balloon almost 30

Golf at the North Pole

degrees to the wind direction no matter what the conditions while also controlling the speed.

It is possible that, given the numerous setbacks there had been in trials, most enthusiasts would have called the whole thing off, but two factors continued to fuel Andree's madness.

The first was that Sweden's subordinate neighbour, Norway, was basking in the success of Nansen who had just returned from his triumphant survival of three years in the Arctic, and the second was Andree's powers of oratory and persuasion. At a lecture to the Royal Swedish Academy of Sciences in 1895 he thrilled his audience with his description of the venture and he was awarded funding from not only the Academy but also Alfred Nobel, the manufacturer of dynamite and the donor of the famous Prizes, and, most importantly, his King, Oscar II. He needed, in today's money, a million dollars and each of the sponsors subscribed a third of this amount. Because of the novels of Jules Verne (especially *Around the World in 80 days, published 1873)* the idea of a balloon journey to the North Pole caught everyone's imagination: if Jules Verne's protagonist could succeed, well, why not our own Swedish hero?

Probably 'starstruck' by his increasing international celebrity status, and now fully funded, he bought a balloon from the Parisian manufacturer Henri Lachambre. The balloon was 67 feet in diameter and had three layers of varnished silk supporting it. Andree christened it the *Ornen* (the Swedish word for *Eagle).*

Thanks to one of the main Swedish newspapers, *Aftonbladet* , he was getting enormous publicity and when his train left Stockholm on the first leg of the journey to Svalbard so much interest had been shown by the public that contemporary illustrations show a railway platform packed with thousands of well-wishers.

As his crew for this 1896 attempt, he had chosen an experienced Arctic meteorologist, Nils Gustaf Ekholm, and a brilliant young student of the sciences and photography, Nils Strindberg.

Andree was an optimistic enthusiast. He was obviously one of these people who felt that whatever he wanted would certainly happen as long as he 'wished' hard enough; he was blind to failure. Floating about in the Arctic sky in a virtually uncontrollable balloon filled with hydrogen depended totally on wind and quite simply there were no other variables. This was his reason for appointing a meteorologist to the crew and Ekholm, the man he picked, was one of the best. He may certainly have been 'the best' of the time, but that time was 1896, not a hundred or so years later when a huge bank of records and satellite imagery were available. Since the weather was the most important risk factor, Ekholm was going to have to forecast not only wind direction but also wind speed. And a further complicating factor was that for the expedition to be successful and for the balloon to be blown over the Pole that special wind would have to blow from the south constantly for 30 days.

The most obvious problem that Andree faced however-- but hoped would 'go away'-- was the fact that the prevailing wind from Svalbard was from the north not the south. But Andree was not discouraged. He was such a willful optimist that because he wanted the wind to blow from the south, it would do so!

On their first trip to Svalbard they built a balloon house, which was basically a framework in which the balloon could be held while the hydrogen-making apparatus filled it with gas. While Andree apparently showed no concerns, expecting the wind to change direction at any moment, Ekholm became increasingly worried.

It became obvious to him, as he watched the balloon being filled with hydrogen, that there was a lot of leakage through the stitch holes and by his calculations, the balloon would never stay filled long enough for them to reach the Pole never mind get to the other side of the Arctic safely. They constantly varnished and glued the eight million tiny stitching holes along the seams but no amount of sealing seemed to stop the leaks that would see them crash unless they could stop it.

Andree had reckoned on the balloon being airborne with the hydrogen load for 30 days, but Ekholm estimated that the longest it could stay airborne for would be 17 days. In the event, because of the unaltered wind direction they had to abort that first attempt and went home to Sweden for the winter.

During the voyage home Ekholm announced that the whole venture was just too dangerous and he was pulling out; his decision had been reinforced when one of the engineers told him that he had seen Andree, from time to time, secretly ordering unscheduled further topping-up of the balloon with hydrogen.

This was a major blow because Ekholm was well-respected and, apart from wanting to live, he had no ulterior motive in resigning from the expedition. He offered to continue with the project but not in the 'leaky' balloon they had taken to Svalbard. His observation was very real and had he pressed the matter, he could probably have received further support from other engineers, but he didn't want to spoil Andree's dream; he simply didn't feel like dying!

So why didn't Andree listen a little more attentively? Probably because he was caught between a rock and a hard place. He had been given a million dollars from the King, the Academy of Sciences and Alfred Nobel and was the focus of Swedish and also world interest.

The situation he found himself in was that an expert had pulled out of the trip, telling him he had to buy another balloon for another third of a million. Did he abort the mission and suffer tremendous shame or should he try to raise another third of a million to buy another balloon?

He chose to do neither and he replaced Ekholm with a 27 year old engineer, Knut Fraenkel. This was a clever choice. Andree was by this time 45 years of age and had no experience or conditioning for a trek over ice should it be necessary but by choosing Fraenkel and Strinberg, he now had two young fit men to help him survive should they crash.

They went back to Svalbard in the summer of 1897 to find that the balloon house had survived the winter well and the wind was at last blowing from the south-west. On 11 July, the explorers climbed into the basket, which

Golf at the North Pole

had been filled with 3000 kilograms of food, scientific equipment, cameras and ballast; on top of this, the balloon was also carrying three large Swedes, so the load was enormous. The top of the balloon hangar was dismantled, the balloon was freed and off they flew.

At first they rose slowly and smoothly, but very soon the several hundred metre long drag ropes were snagging on the ground and dragging the basket dangerously close to the sea. To try and gain height and lessen the strain on the guide ropes, the crew dumped over 200 kilograms of ballast -- but this wasn't enough. The strain became too great for the ropes and rather than disentangling from the ground obstacles, they tore off from their attachments to the basket. With this further loss of weight - 500 kilograms of rope - the balloon shot up into the air quite uncontrollably, turning it from a theoretically steerable vessel into an ordinary hydrogen balloon at the mercy of the wind with insufficient ballast. It rapidly rose to 700 metres and to the horror of the watchers on the shore, it quickly disappeared from sight.

That was the last seen of them until August 1930, some 33 years later, when their remains were found by a Norwegian Bratvaag expedition that was studying the glaciers and seas of the Svalbard archipelago. The island of Kvitoya was usually inaccessible to the ships of the time because it was almost permanently surrounded by a thick sheet of ice, but 1930 was a warm year and the Norwegian scientists took the opportunity to explore a seldom visited island of the archipelago. They first found a boat frozen under a mound of snow and full of food and equipment and then they found a journal and two skeletal remains identified from their clothing as Andree and Strinberg. While most of Strinberg remained there was very little of Andre because polar bears had eaten his head and limbs!

Once news of this discovery reached Sweden, the newspaper proprietors combined to charter a sealing sloop to take their reporters and investigators to the island and they landed on 5 September. After a short search they found a third body, Fraenkel, buried in a shallow grave. They also found a tin box containing Strinberg's film, logbook and maps, which they presented to the Swedish Academy.

The bodies were taken back to Sweden, arriving in Stockholm on 5 October, where they were cremated without any further autopsy.

From their journals and from the 93 of 240 photographs taken by Strinberg that the Royal Institute of Technology in Stockholm were able to save, we now know what happened to them.

After floating out of sight of the ground crew, they settled into steady flight dropping three of their cork message containers, two of which were later found. These indicated that at that point in time all was well and that 'spirits were high'.

According to Andree's main diary however things soon started going wrong with the balloon out of equilibrium and furthermore, since it was far higher than planned, the hydrogen was leaking out too quickly. Free flight continued for ten and a half hours after which they had a horrendous period of 40 hours during which the balloon was completely out of control bumping along the

Golf at the North Pole

ice, rotating and yawing, causing them all to suffer from motion sickness. Finally they crashed on to the ice.

They had travelled for 2 days and 3 hours during which time according to Andree no one had managed any sleep.

Fortunately the landing was relatively gentle and they were able to unload the basket and set up camp. They had guns, snow shoes, skis, a tent, sledges and a small boat. What was a complete disaster was their clothing. Like many other older expeditions they had not studied the Inuit ways of survival in the North and although they had oilskins, their underlying woolen clothes were always sodden and wet and could not be dried. Also, instead of using Inuit flexible sledges, which could be pulled across the ridges, Andree had constructed rigid sleds, which proved very difficult to handle over the rough terrain.

Before they even attempted to walk back to safety, they very sensibly stayed in the tent for a week while they planned what to do. They reckoned that the nearest land was Franz Joseph Land and they planned to walk there over the ice.

Their lack of Arctic knowledge and preparation, however, saw them lurch from disaster to disaster. Their initial error was to load each sledge with 200 kilograms of equipment and provisions, which made them far too heavy to drag, a fact that became quickly obvious, especially over rough ice. After a week, they dropped the loads to 130 kilograms, but this was still too heavy for untrained men, especially the relatively aged Andree.

After a few days they discovered, as most other Arctic explorers did, that Arctic ice drifts: so that as they went forwards, they were actually being carried backwards, the all too frequent problem that even the most experienced Arctic travellers have no answer for.

After two weeks they realised that getting to Franz Josef Land was going to be beyond them and so they aimed for the Svalbard archipelago, which had been their original starting point. The first few days of travel went well and they were able to use their boat over large leads of water and shoot plenty of walrus and polar bear, but the fates turned against them once again; once they were on the ice they found that the drift was taking them back the way they had come.

By the beginning of September they had resigned themselves to wintering on the ice and Strinberg drew up plans for a winter hut made of water reinforced snow. It was planned to have three rooms -- a storeroom, a room with a table in it and a three sleeping bag bedroom. Since they were drifting south very fast Andree recorded that it might be that they could feed themselves adequately from the sea.

At first things went well and they constructed their snow house, but on 2 October the floe began to break up directly underneath them and they were forced to evacuate quickly onto the rocky shore of Kvitoya Island with their supplies. This took a couple of days, but all seemed to be well because in his diary Andree wrote

"Morale remains good. With comrades such as these, one ought to be able to manage under practically any circumstances whatsoever"

Golf at the North Pole

But within a few days of writing that, all three men were dead.

If one looks at the rough drawings made by Strindberg for their winter house with three rooms, we are not looking at men at the end of their tether with illnesses such as scurvy, starvation or exposure. No one had gangrene or frostbite and they had had sufficient food. The winter had not yet arrived and that was shown by the fact that the ice floe on which they had built their hut had cracked -- a thing it would not have done had the temperature dropped to winter levels.

We do not know how long they survived on the shore line of Kvitoya island, where they were found, but we do know that Fraenkel died first because he was buried, meaning that the other two must have been strong enough to man-handle his corpse. But there was no sign that they had built a shelter or another 'winter house' and they had certainly left a lot of their equipment and provisions on the shore.

Ernst Tryde, a medical practitioner, wrote the book entitled *The Dead on Kvitoya* in 1952 in which he postulated that the men had died from eating undercooked polar bear meat thus contracting a disease known as Trichinosis (one of the bits of evidence he used for this was the finding of the larvae of *Trichinella Spiralis*, the infecting organism, in polar bear remains nearby). This claim however has survived the passage of time no better than the numerous other medical articles in which physicians attempt to guess the illnesses and causes of death of other worthies such as Mozart, Bach and Beethoven.

One factor against a diagnosis of Trichinosis is that Arctic explorers have survived by eating polar bear meat cooked and uncooked on numerous expeditions and while it might have been possible that one of the party suffered Trichinosis, for this disease to have caused three deaths in such a short time is unbelievable. Furthermore Trichinosis is not an acute disease and people can live with it for years.

In 2010 this Trichinosis theory was rejected by a researcher from the prestigious Karolinska Institute in Stockholm who favoured the theory that Strinberg had been killed by a polar bear. We have seen this happen tragically to an English schoolboy in Svalbard in 2011, but in this instance, all three had guns at their sides and had shot polar bears at least every week. It is probable however that bits of Strinberg and a lot of Andree were eaten by a polar bear after they were dead.

The fact that all journal and diary entries ended at the same time and that three relatively fit men (two young and one middle-aged) died at virtually the same time in the same place would make me favour a diagnosis of acute vitamin A toxicity.

Megadoses of vitamins are harmless apart from vitamins A,D and B6. Vitamin A is normally bound to a protein in the body but when all this protein is used up, the excess unbound vitamin damages cell membranes and is usually fatal unless a liver is transplanted.

Since the 1940's it has been known that the liver of polar bears, and to a lesser extent seals, contain large amounts of vitamin A. While some polar explorers would only use the meat of the bear some might use the liver and kidneys to make a stew and it is this group who are at risk. The initial symptoms would be headaches and dermatitis but acute liver failure and death follow.

It has been suggested that Andree was a victim of the publicity with which he had surrounded himself. In those days there were no smooth public relations men to turn any crisis into an advantage.

Andree needed a new balloon! The abandonment of the expedition on those grounds would today have been presented by a skilled public relations expert as a 'technological breakthrough that potentially had saved hundreds of lives and that had it not been for Andree's pioneering work he would almost certainly have not only lost his life but the lives of his companions'. But this was the end of the nineteenth not the twentieth century. Had Andree pulled out, he would have been disgraced.

Together with Bear Grylls, David Hempleman-Adams is probably Britain's foremost adventurer. In 2000, he became the first man to fly over the North Pole in a balloon, adding this to his numerous other accomplishments. He has made many other epic balloon journeys, including one across the Atlantic from New Brunswick, Canada, to Blackpool - another first.

I asked Dan which gasses were used today.

'Did you never read about the Hindenburg disaster when the world's biggest airship caught fire as it was landing at Lakehurst, New Jersey in 1937? Well that was the end of hydrogen and what's used now is helium because that doesn't burn".

The type of balloon used now for long distance flights is the Roziere balloon, which uses both heated and unheated lifting gases.

But Andree did not have these choices. He might however have been better advised to have closely examined the balloon before he parted with his money to the Paris balloon manufacturer. It was leakier than it should have been.

It wasn't because of this story that I didn't take the tied balloon flight captained by Dan.

It just wasn't worth the money.

Chapter 17
The Royal Explorer

I was discussing the history of Italy with the two former steel executives, Gian Carlo and Maurizio, both of whom agreed with my view that Garibaldi hadn't made a very good job of making a country when he united Italy in 1861. Both were northerners and were rather tepid supporters of The Northern League party that wants the North to separate from the South.

Gian Carlo said 'I'm a Venetian; I live in Rome but I'm a Venetian. The only time I'm Italian is when I watch football.' Maurizio concurred, saying, 'I'm from Torino and to tell you the truth I'd rather be French or Swiss than Italian'. They both shared the same view as to the twin evils of present day Italy -- the Vatican and Berlusconi.

I disagreed about Berlusconi. 'Italy has only ever had three leaders,' I argued. 'Garibaldi, Mussolini and Berlusconi. The rest of the time it has been a shambles. In fact it's been an example to the rest of the world that if you have a creative, vibrant population you have no need of a government'. There was a bit of humming and hawing about this but they did give some qualified support to Mussolini's leadership from 1922 until at least 1940, when he chose the wrong side to support in the war.

By this time we were sailing through the pack ice and as we looked out on the foggy wilderness Gian Carlo said 'Let me tell you two Arctic stories, one about a Fascist and one about a non-Fascist.'

He didn't know if the Duke of Abruzzi was a card carrying member of the Party or not, but from his willingness to take an official position in the Italian rule of Somalia when it was invaded in the 1930s one must presume that he at least went along with the fascist idea of creating an Italian Empire in Africa.

He had flawless royal connections, being the nephew of King Vittorio Emanuele II, who became the second King of Italy in 1878. His father Amedeo, Vittorio Emanuele's brother, had been King of Spain, but on the unification of Italy he abdicated and returned to Italy to become part of the royal household, taking the title Duke of Aosta.

When christened, the Duke of Abruzzi was given a very long name -- Luigi Amedeo Giuseppe Maria Ferdinando Francesco di Savoia.

Gian Carlo pronounced this mellifluously in one breath.

Although Luigi, from his photographs, looks the epitome of a pre-First World War European aristocrat -- slicked back black hair, hooked nose, curly moustache and a monocle-- he was a cut above most of the other spineless individuals who swanned around the pleasure palaces of the European Courts in the late nineteenth century.

Between 1893 and 1896 he travelled widely and spent a considerable time honing his mountaineering techniques in the Alps. He developed sufficient expertise to take on harder climbs and in fact became the first to climb Mount St Elias in Canada in 1897.

He was enormously popular in Italy because, as a new nation, they were looking for heroes. In the Edwardian era, even in Italy, heroism was the name of the game; the working class looked for heroes to emerge from their 'betters' and poets also hyped the market. This concept of course was completely exhausted after the horrors of the First World War but at that time in Italy, the young royal adventurer looked like the real ticket; he was the fresh face of Italy ... had *Hello* magazine been published at that time, he might have been a 'cover-boy'.

As the nineteenth century was coming to an end he decided to explore the Arctic. It was a popular subject and talked about in every context and medium. Nansen was probably one of the best-recognised people in the world and Andree and his friends had recently disappeared off the face of the earth in their balloon in rather spectacular fashion.

Luigi was 26 when he went to pay respects to and meet Nansen in Oslo. He arrived one day, unannounced, at Nansen's front door and set out to learn as much as he could from the great man. He arrived with some basic knowledge of survival in icy conditions at high altitudes from his mountaineering experiences; his climbing expertise would also be useful if and when his party were faced with ice hummocks. But learning how to survive in the Arctic required more time than a chat over a cup of tea.

But with the confidence of one 'born to rule', six months later he was on his way to the Pole. Of course if you don't need sponsors and can fund the whole thing yourself, it cuts down the time normally required for the preparation of an expedition.

He purchased a 570 ton whaling ship and re christened it the *Stella Polare* and recruited a crew half of whom were Italian and the other half Norwegian. Among the Italians were men who were professional Alpine guides and were therefore young, fit and strong.

He identified Archangel in Russia as his favoured point of departure because this was the place that claimed to sell the most suitable dogs; unfortunately he bought the dogs unseen and when he arrived he found he had been duped-- the dogs were of variable and poor quality; but he had bought 120 of them and once there, there was little he could do about it.

His plan was to sail from Archangel to Franz Josef Land, where he aimed to set up his winter quarters on Cape Flora , which had at one time served as Frederick Jackson's winter quarters and where Nansen and Johansen were taken when they first came across Jackson. These huts were still intact and habitable. Once there he planned to sail as far north as the ship would allow and from that point start to send out relay parties over the ice with the aim of laying down supply depots for the group that would make the final attempt.

Golf at the North Pole

He had been selective in taking Nansen's advice. While he had enthusiastically taken up Nansen's designs for sledges and kayaks, he hadn't listened when Nansen talked about the importance of the correct clothing. This was unfortunate because Nansen had started with the traditional woolens but had quickly learned from the Inuits the importance of fur and animal skins. In some ways we should understand that dressing in the clothes of the Inuit would be to people like Abruzzi 'dressing like a savage and not a gentleman'.

He also ignored Nansen's advice about skis; this wasn't clever. The ski-ing that he thought he knew about wasn't the ski-ing that Nansen was talking about. Italian Dukes skied downhill and Norwegians skied cross country, and since it was the early days of skiing he didn't fully appreciate the important difference between the ski design needed for each. As well as the ski design and bindings, he had not appreciated what Nansen had told him about different types of waxes for different conditions. Skis prepared for wet snow will not glide across dry snow and vice versa. In fairness however perhaps Abruzzi knew that he didn't have enough skiing experience to suddenly adopt new techniques when there was so much else to learn -- but half his crew was Norwegian and some of them would have had this knowledge. He also had to take into account that there would be a lot of climbing over hummocks and ridges and in this situation skis would be a handicap.

Because he was a 'Royal' there was a lot of fuss when he arrived in Archangel. Instead of having time to prepare, train dogs and finalise the loading of stores and equipment, he had to do the diplomatic rounds with all the neighbouring diplomats who had descended on the town in order to present their country's greetings to the relative of the Italian King.

When he was finally released from meetings demanded by protocol he took his ship up the Davina river and aimed for Franz Josef Land arriving there four days later and anchoring at Prince Rudolf island (the northernmost island of the archipelago). From there he moved on to the ice pack and started his depot-laying expeditions. However, soon afterwards, as winter advanced, the *Stella Polare,* his ship, was crushed and holed by ice pressure and had to be evacuated. Winter was unexpectedly early that year because this happened by 9 September 1899, an unusually early time for ice of that density. To someone of Royal blood this looked bad, but to someone of a more practical nature, his Captain, Umberto Cagni, it was just another problem to be fixed.

Most Polar explorers would probably have been keen Boy Scouters had the movement existed when they were young. They were quite happy to 'rough it' lying in a tent on the ice in a sleeping bag that may or may not have to be shared by another person. But this way of living was not what 'Royals' did.

Abruzzi never even considered 'roughing it'. He had brought along a system of three tents which, when constructed, gave him a triple insulated fully functioning Arctic pavilion.

The first tent was covered by a second tent and these two formed the living quarters. These two tents were then covered by a huge third tent. The living quarters had camp beds, feather mattresses, wooden floors and

Golf at the North Pole

stoves. The galley occupied the space between the inner and middle tents and the stores were between the middle and outer tents. It was so effective that even when the stoves were turned off at night the temperature never sank below zero

Just as expected, Cagni fixed the damage to the *Stella Polare* but then another problem arose. Abruzzi and Cagni, while out laying down stores and depots, lost their way in a storm as they were going back to the tents on 23 December and fell into a lead; they managed to get out, but by the time they had returned to the camp, soaking wet, Luigi had frostbite on his fingers and the expedition doctor had to remove some tips. Unfortunately that ruled him out of being in the party that was going to march to the Pole.

A lesser man might have been put out by this but Abruzzi was a team player and thereafter put all his efforts into making sure that at least some of the team reached the Pole. He did not have the selfish personal ambition of some of the other polar explorers who were doing it exclusively for their own egos. He put Cagni, a man he knew well since they had climbed Mount St Elias together, in charge of all operational matters.

Umberto Cagni was a ship's captain and, as such, good at man management ; he chose as his colleagues for the polar attempt his Lieutenant, Francesco Querini, and the expedition doctor, Cavalli Molinelli. Abruzzi stepped back and gave his number two his full support and encouragement. In fact he wrote in his diary "I could not have entrusted the expedition to a leader more gifted with energy and activity, more prompt at finding expedients or endowed with greater moral and physical endurance." Certainly with what was to follow Abruzzi was not wrong.

On 11 March 1900, Cagni left the luxurious royal camp along with 10 men, 102 dogs and 13 sledges. Like all polar expeditions they carried pemmican, tinned goods and a substance called 'lightweight carbohydrate', better known today as 'pasta'. They wore insulated Nordic footwear called *finneskos* so that they could run alongside the overloaded sledges to keep pace with the dogs.

Unforunately they wore the usual European woolens with all the attendant disadvantages. Cagni wrote that in temperatures of minus 80 degrees, their clothing became like an armour of ice encasing them, and largely because of this, each day they lost many hours merely getting decamped.

In Cagni's party were three very fit young Alpine guides, Simone Canepa, Alessio Fenouillet and Guiseppe Petigax. As they moved north and the conditions became worse they decided to cut down on rations, but it quickly became obvious that if conditions did not dramatically improve they were not going to get near the North Pole anyway. Bearing this in mind - and hoping to achieve something from the expedition - they pressed on until 24 April when, at 86 degrees 33 minutes north, they gave up. Getting this far gave them the 'furthest north' record - they had beaten Nansen by 21 miles - but with the temperature at 60 degrees below they felt they would be lucky to get back never mind go even a mile further. As a celebration, which they considered might be their last,

Golf at the North Pole

they drank all the brandy in the medicine box and did not recover from their hangovers till noon the next day!

When they turned back, initially the going was easy, but after a few days they found that they had travelled 90 miles south, which meant that if that progress continued they would be able to reach the *Stella Polaris* before the end of May.

But by now Cagni had a frostbitten finger.

Frostbite is due to the blood supply to the periphery of a hand or foot being closed down due to the cold for such a period that the tissues it should supply with oxygen, die; dead tissue has no immunity against what are called commensal bacteria, the bacteria we have on our bodies all the time but which are kept at bay by our immune system. Dead tissue often also gets infected by bacteria such as *Clostridiium welschii* which causes gas gangrene, a condition which creates pus, death of tissue and an absolutely unforgettably awful smell.

Gangrene is one of the reasons that surgical diplomas were first issued to Naval surgeons. Centuries ago if a soldier was wounded by rifle or shell fire on the battlefield, he would be left to die, and eventually his rotting corpse would fertilise the field in which he lay.

In the Navy however it was different. If a sailor got a cannon wound and didn't die, his wound would almost certainly go gangrenous. Several weeks later he might die but in those days the smell of the rotting gangrene would make life intolerable for the rest of the crew on the ship and so amputation of the affected limb would have to be performed. Surgeons were thus taught how to amputate a limb (without a general anaesthetic) in the shortest possible time -- not primarily to save a life, but to stop the smell!

The other bacterium that lives in dead tissue is *Pseudomonas Pyocyaneus* which has an even worse smell. It is so bad that if a surgeon gets any pus contaminated with this on his skin then he will have to wash the area many times before the smell disappears.

It is a unique experience to be anywhere near a gangrenous wound. It is an unforgettable and absolutely nauseous odour and it was possibly an explanation for Captain Oates' colleagues not stopping him from walking out of the Scott expedition tent into a blizzard.

So there was Cagni smelling like an abandoned cesspit or worse. And what did he do? He amputated his finger himself -- but he was left on his own to do the operation because the others had to leave the tent for the two hours it took him because they couldn't watch!

The affected finger was on his right hand and so he had to 'operate' with his left hand. What might have taken a surgeon with training three minutes, took Cagni two hours; but when he had finished, his companions were once again able to enter the tent. In his diary he describes how, when his initial incision was made, pus erupted 'as if from a volcano'. But then he had to cut most of the dead tissue off and without someone (or another hand) to hold it taut so the knife could cut, he must have suffered the most awful pain for those two hours in which he was cutting off his finger millimeter by millimeter.

The next day they covered 18 miles and he noted in his diary that he was in great pain but did not mention it to his companions because "it seems to me that yesterday's operation rather upset them"

As they kept going south the conditions were good and things were going as well as could be expected until Cagni took a measure of the longitude. He was about to discover the curse of all polar expeditions -- drift. They were now miles west of Prince Rudolph Island and were being carried by the polar drift; it was as if they were on a treadmill that spun faster than they could walk. They continued trying to overcome this problem merely by trying to march faster than the 'treadmill', until by 7 June, they reckoned that in the previous seven days, they had advanced only three feet!.

Also, by now, the summer thaw was well underway, and with the ice and snow turning to slush, conditions for travel on foot were getting almost impossible. In some places the slush would disguise a water hole into which they'd plunge; and so they continued-- slow, wet and frozen.

Then they saw land. It seemed to be only about 10 miles away but the Arctic light was playing tricks with them. This illusion has been reported by many polar explorers and is akin to the mirages seen by travellers in the desert. They kept expecting to arrive at the coastline they could clearly see but they never seemed to get closer; it was another 7 days of almost constant travel before they reached the safe solid ice surrounding Harley Island at the northern tip of Franz Josef Land. During this time their food supplies were running dangerously low and so they marched with few stops, little sleep and only one food stop per day. Although they were now on land and no longer drifting, they were still many miles away from the safety of their base on Prince Rudolph Island. They continued travelling 20 hours a day; the three Alpine guides, fit young men, were able to keep this up but Cagni, a sea captain and only an amateur mountaineer, was near collapse and had to ride on a sledge. But they made it; on 23 June they crossed a hill and saw below them the *Stella Polare*.

They arrived with no stores, broken sledges, bits of kayaks, no sleeping bags and their clothes in rags. But there was bad news waiting for them, One of the two depot laying teams that they'd sent back before the final push had not returned to base and were missing.

Abruzzi had then to take a hard decision -- did he stay for another winter searching for the missing party or should he go home. The chances of finding two men who had already been missing for 3 months with the ice breaking up was minimal and so he made the difficult decision to abandon them and aim for home.

The *Stella Polare* at this point was caught in ice and although the damage had been repaired it had not yet been tested at sea and more might require to be done. In order to free the ship from its icy bed he laid 70 mines of gun cotton and gunpowder into the 17 foot thick ice that was imprisoning his boat and literally blew the ship out of the ice. Fortunately the repairs that Cagni had carried out had been successful, no more required to be done, the ship was seaworthy and they sailed for home, arriving in Tromso, Norway, on 6 September from where

Golf at the North Pole

Abruzzi sent two telegrams-- one to his cousin, the new King, and one to Nansen.

They had reached 'furthest North' and so had created a record, but the price was six deaths. The success of the expedition however was to prove to the geographic community that the Americans had the right idea of where the starting point of a Polar expedition should be -- and it wasn't Franz Josef Land which is too far away and the drifts are never favourable. Another reason not to start from Franz Josef Land is that the ice there becomes too thick. Although that might have been true at one time because when Abruzzi was there the ice was 17 feet thick; when I was there, there was virtually none!

I asked Gian Carlo what happened to Abruzzi when Italy was taken over by the Fascists in 1922. Apparently he ignored politics and went on climbing, leading a successful mountaineering expedition to Ruwenzori Range in Uganda, and to K2 in Karakorum, Mongolia. He was honoured by every major exploring and geographic society and died while a serving diplomat in Mogadishu in Italian Somaliland in 1933.

Having heard the story I said to Gian Carlo 'That's very interesting but the Fascist Party hadn't been invented at the that time he went to the Pole'

'But' he replied 'had it been, he would have been part of it. Ever since the start of the Fascist Party the royal family has supported them (at least until 1944) and in 1922 it was the King who had deposed the current Prime Minister to appoint Mussolini. I've no doubt he subscribed to the Fascist cause'.

185

'So what's the story about the anti-Fascist?' I asked

Although the sun was now shining at midnight he slipped down the last of his vodka and told me I'd have to wait till the next evening to hear about Umberto Nobile.

Chapter 18
The Red Tent

'If the Italian 'Royals' did so well, how come you got rid of the monarchy?' I asked.

'The war', replied Maurizio. 'People don't realise that modern Italy was not made during the Renaissance, not during the Garibaldi years and not during Mussolini's time. It was created between 1943 and 1946'.

This was a concept that was new to me and I asked Maurizio to expand. As he did so he smiled and explained that Gian Carlo was 'right' and he was 'left' -- politically.

'But that's the story of Italy today. You are either right wing or left wing and to change your allegiance would be tantamount to undergoing a sex change. Both sides have long given up on any hope that Italian politicians will do anything other than make things worse so we have our opinions and live on. But we share a cabin'.

He continued, 'As Italy picked up the bits after the War it now consisted of an anticlerical communist/left North and a God fearing Catholic conservative South. There were a few more northerners than southerners when they held a referendum to decide the future of the monarchy, and when they decided against, the King and his family got on a plane at Ciampino airport in 1946 and went into exile'.

But when they started to tell me about Nobile, they went back not to the Second World War but the First.

It was 1925. Amundsen, the greatest explorer ever, was getting too old to put his body through weeks of torture, skiing/walking to the North Pole; but he thought that now, with the new technology of flight, he might get there the easy way, by plane.

He persuaded the American philanthropist Lloyd Ellsworth to fund an attempt to fly over the North Pole in two Dornier Flying boats. With three men in each plane they flew to 87 degrees north and all was looking good until both planes were forced to land due to bad weather and fortunately, even though they had lost radio contact, the crews managed to reunite. One of the flying boats was damaged in the landing meaning that the remaining plane would have to attempt a take-off with twice the normal load since it had to carry six rather than three people. That meant a very long landing strip had to be prepared and so the six men started digging and shovelling in the hope that they had prepared something long enough to avoid another crash.

Rather surprisingly, the experienced Amundsen had not taken into consideration that he might be stranded and might need survival rations, and so the six men had to move 600 tons of ice and snow in 30 days while on starvation rations. Fortunately the plane got off the ground and they all arrived back in Svalbard safely.

Nearly getting himself killed on that journey did not deter the indomitable Norwegian. He persuaded the generous Ellsworth to dip into his pockets again so that he could make another attempt the next year; but this time he reckoned it was safer using an airship rather than a small plane, because it could carry much greater loads.

By 1925 the public accepted that Amundsen had reached the South Pole; even Scott had confirmed it because he had seen Amundsen's tent and flag; so there was no argument.

But there was still doubt about the North Pole. Byrd's flight records were still disputed by some, and the Peary-Cook controversy (chapter 19) had left many still harbouring doubts. So Amundsen still had something to prove by going north.

In the 1920s the best airships were being made in Italy and the best designer was Umberto Nobile who had a factory just north of Rome at Bracciano employing 1200 workers (there is still a beautiful aeronautics museum there with many Nobile artifacts). In the first war Italy was at the forefront of airship design and they had managed to hold on to that position in peacetime. This was probably because Britain, France and America were concentrating on aeroplane development rather than airship design.

When Amundsen first contacted him, Nobile's mind was not entirely on airship design because he was under political threat. In 1922 Mussolini had taken over power and instituted a climate of confrontation within society that said 'if you're not with us you're against us' and while the main target of this challenge were communist sympathisers it remained a general threat.

Nobile was well known for his left wing sympathies and this made him an enemy of the Fascists; and even though he held a commission in the Italian Air Force, they started to harass him, trying to get him to resign from airship design and turn over his factory to the Government for aeroplane development. As a result of this pressure he sought relief for a short period by translocating to America where he became a consultant to the Goodyear tyre company; but in less than a year he returned to Italy

'You obviously know Italy ' said Maurizio 'and you realise that every part of life is a contest. You know that since the end of the war, 66 Governments have ruled. Even today, who you know counts for far more than what you know. Connections are everything, and Nobile did not have the connections that his rival manufacturer in the airship design business, General Gaetano Crocco, had'.

Although Nobile held an equivalent rank in the Italian Air Force to Crocco, the latter was in the Fascist Party and had the ear of General Italo Balbo, Chief of the Air Force Defence Staff. Balbo wanted no more time and money put into airship design since he wanted to follow Britain and America in developing aeroplanes.

It is easy to see Nobile as the victim in this situation but since he later emigrated to Stalin's Russia, one must presume that his communist sympathies were strong, and this would have been totally unacceptable to the Fascist Party which saw itself as Italy's saviour from Communism. Also, his rehabilitation immediately after the end of the Second World War reflected the wishes of the then powerful Partisans most of whom were Communists, underpinned by the philosophy of "my enemy's enemy must be my friend" and vice-versa.

But he was still in business when he was summoned to Oslo by Amundsen who asked him to build an airship to overfly the North Pole within a year. At the time, Nobile was planning an airship called the *N-1* but he considered it too heavy for an Arctic flight and suggested to Amundsen that he design a new custom- built model. But Amundsen was impatient; he was 53 years of age and realised his polar days were coming to an end and wanted one last visit to the snow and ice wilderness that he loved so much.

Nobile therefore set about modifying the *N-1* for long-range flying in cold weather. He accomplished this within the year and on 29 March 1926 an official hand-over ceremony was arranged at Ciampino airport in Rome. With drums beating and bands playing, Mussolini was all set to take a prominent role in the handover ceremony even though Amundsen had made it quite clear that since it was being paid for and controlled by Norwegian and American money, the Italians had no place in the venture. They had merely designed what Amundsen had ordered and paid for. And as if to rub in,

Amundsen insisted that the name of the airship be changed from *N-1* to *Norge*.

But Mussolini loved ceremonies, wearing medals and sashes, and giving speeches, and so he would have been very disappointed that the ceremony, over which he was to preside, was abandoned because of a thunderstorm. A week later, without *Il Duce's* presence, the airship took off from Rome for a 17 hour flight to Leningrad. It was piloted by Nobile and apart from the mechanics and the rigger, all the crew were Scandanavian.

From Leningrad they flew to Svalbard from where they set off on the polar attempt on 11 May. Less than 24 hours later it was 'mission accomplished'; they were overflying the Pole. At this point there was an important piece of ceremonial to be performed; Norwegian, American and Italian flags were dropped from the airship onto the ice, but relations between Amundsen and Nobile, which had become strained in the freezing, cramped and noisy gondola, became even worse, when Amundsen saw that the Italian flag dropped was much larger than any of the others.

Amundsen later recalled with scorn that under Nobile, the airship had become "a circus wagon in the sky"; Nobile had even brought along his little dog Titania, as a mascot

After crossing the Pole, ice encrustations kept growing on the airship to such an extent that the large pieces of ice which broke off were blown into the hull by the propellers making multiple small perforations in the covering.

Golf at the North Pole

On 14 May the airship reached the Inuit village of Teller in Alaska, where, in view of worsening weather, the decision was made to land, rather than continue to Nome, their original destination.

After the expedition, relations between Amundsen and Nobile became even worse, because Nobile found it politic to obey Mussolini's order to go on a lecture tour of the United States emphasising that the success of overflying the North Pole was due to Italian engineering expertise rather than Amundsen's courage. It's hard to find fault with this because Amundsen and Ellsworthy contributed nothing to this venture other than money, and it was Nobile's well designed airship and command that had completed the journey.

The lecture tour of America must have gone a long way to boosting Nobile's self confidence because he began to conceive of a repeat venture that would be entirely Italian, with an Italian leader, an Italian airship, Italian money and an all-Italian crew.

It was the nineteen twenties and Mussolini had overcome every problem at home; he was on the verge of making peace between the Government and the Pope for the first time since 1860, he was promoting Italy's greatness to the world, he was about to expand an Italian Empire in Africa---- but he drew the line at supporting the 'Communist' airman who wanted to do 'great things'. If Nobile had not been well known world wide he would have suffered the fate of many other opponents of the regime and been 'disappeared', but this was impossible. Another black mark against Nobile was that he continued to cause grief within the ranks of the Air Force by refusing to abandon airships and move his factory on to the development of aeroplanes.

While Nobile's left wing attitudes were obviously unacceptable to the Fascist Party they were unable to keep him starved of the oxygen of publicity. They did not want him to undertake the journey but on the other hand they could not forbid it, because the eyes of the world were on Nobile and for the moment he was 'the Star'. They gave very little help, and what help they did give was in bad grace.

Not fully appreciating the power of a well-organised party machine, Nobile 'heard' the messages but he wasn't 'listening' to what was really being intimated and it nearly cost both him and his crew their lives. He kept pushing ahead with his plans, countering every block put in his way and ignoring the threats and intimidation to himself and his staff. The only thing that saved him from being destroyed by the Party was his immense popularity with the public.

He managed to build an N-class airship and using the lessons learned from his first flight, he was very confident that this one would be even more successful and that not only would he be able to fly to the Pole but he'd be able to turn around and fly back to base.

While the government limited itself to funding the construction of the airship, they refused any further help. Nobile, still trying to curry some favour with the Fascists, christened his new airship, *Italia,* but the funding for the equipment and crew came from the city of Milan and that shamed the government into sending a support steamship re-named *Citta di Milano*. They also took the precaution of putting it under the captaincy of a faithful Fascist Party member, Captain Guiseppe Romagna.

As the Fascist Party realised that they were not going to be able to stop this expedition, Balbo, the Air Force chief, is reported to have said, "Let him go, for he cannot possibly come back to bother anyone"

In the light of subsequent events this was the scenario that played out and it is reminiscent of what happened many decades later when Prime Minister Aldo Moro was kidnapped and murdered in Italy in 1974. It was a 'State assassination'

Nobile departed from Milan on 15 April 1928 and flew initially to Stolp and then onto Svalbard with a crew of 18, some of whom had travelled in the *Norge* --and of course his dog Titania

After having to stall for some weeks due to bad weather they were able to take off on 23 May for the North Pole which they reached within a day, this time dropping another Italian flag as well as a crucifix given to them by the Vatican. They did not intend to repeat the Amundsen trip of flying with the wind over the Pole to Alaska or Siberia; they were going to do something that had never been done before -- they were going to fly back to Svalbard. And that was the wrong decision.

As they turned back towards Svalbard, the weather closed in and the ship crashed onto the ice on May 25. The airship broke up and of the sixteen crew, ten were thrown out of the gondola onto the ice, but tragically, the remaining six, trapped in the now lightened shell, were whisked off into the sky never to be seen again. No trace has ever been found of either their remains or remains of the airship which may well have exploded.

Of the ten thrown onto the ice, one died immediately from the trauma, Nobile broke his arm and the chief engineer. Ceccione, who had flown on the *Norge* expedition, broke both of his legs so badly that there was visible displacement of alignment; two others had shoulder and rib injuries.

The gondola had broken off from the body of the airship and so the crew were able to retrieve some material for survival, including a radio receiver and a tent which they later painted red for maximum visibility in the event of rescue attempts. For a month this 'red tent' featured on the front page of newspapers all round the world because it was the perfect story-- find the red dot in the middle of an icy waste and save the occupants who only have a limited time to survive. A day by day story with a possible tragic outcome was just what editors would have ordered.

As the unfortunate six who were not thrown out of the ship were carried off to their deaths, one of them, an engineer called Ettore Arduino, courageously managed to throw out some packages of food and survival clothing. The ice floe that the survivors were on was drifting towards the outer islands of the Svalbard archipelago and so three of the fit men decided to try and walk back to the base so that they could summon help. One was a Swedish meteorologist and the other two were Italians. The Swede 'disappeared' and the two Italians were later picked up by a Russian icebreaker the *Krasin*.

Golf at the North Pole

Even though he had fallen out with Nobile, during and especially after the voyage of the *Norge,* Amundsen, as soon as he heard of the crash, volunteered to lead a search party. He was given a seaplane by the French government together with an experienced pilot; they left on 16 June and were never heard of again.

In Norway you might hear it said that Amundsen found the Italians and they cannibalised him but that is not true! Similar rumours also developed about the two Italians who had set off with the Swedish meteorologist and were subsequently picked up by the Russian ice breaker *Krasin*. The Swede also was supposedly missing because the Italians had eaten him!

In the wake of the crash one of the first international air and sea rescue operations was put into action with contributions from Russia, Norway, Sweden, Finland -- and, reluctantly, Italy. A rich Italian businessman and friend of Nobile, threatened to embarrass Mussolini by funding a rescue attempt himself if the government didn't help; this catalysed some action but it was slow and obviously reluctant.

Nobile's radio operator, Biagi, became the hero of the hour. He set up an aerial and worked round the clock sending out details of their position. These messages were picked up in all the polar countries, but since the radio equipment on the *Citta di Milano* back-up ship was being constantly used 'for recreational purposes' (or so they said) they denied ever hearing from the stranded party. Whether or not they were acting on orders from Rome we do not know, but their abandonment of their countrymen was unforgiveable, and so it was judged by the rest of the world.

By now it was June, and the ice floes were breaking up; time was getting short to get help to the injured men. The Italians had been on the ice in the 'red tent' for a month by the time the first rescue plane arrived. It was a Swedish Air Force Fokker ski plane piloted by Lieutenant Elnar Lundborg. Nobile had prepared an evacuation plan which included getting the badly injured Ceccione off first, himself fourth and Biagi last but Lundborg was having none of it. His instructions were to take only one passenger for the sake of safety and that unarguably was going to be Nobile. While it might have been tempting to construct this as a Fascist plot to damage Nobile, it wasn't; it was definitely a Swedish government decision. When Lundborg came back for the other survivors he crashed as he landed in very difficult circumstances, damaged his plane and had to spend the rest of the time sharing camp with the original survivors

When Nobile reached the *Città di Milano* he was dismayed at the incompetence and indifference that he found. All of his attempts to help co-ordinate the international rescue effort were blocked. When he threatened to leave, he was placed under virtual arrest by Captain Romagna and locked in his cabin. His telegrams to the survivors still on the ice, as well as to various people involved in the rescue, were heavily censored.

It was wrongly reported in Fascist Italian newspapers that his own evacuation was an obvious sign of cowardice. After 48 days on the ice floe, the last five men of his crew were rescued by the Soviet icebreaker *Krasin*

Golf at the North Pole

on 13 July. Nobile insisted that he wanted to continue the search for the six crew who had been swept away in the airship when it disintegrated, but he was ordered back to Rome with the others.

The return to Italy was planned to be a public humiliation of Nobile and his crew. After they had been taken by their support ship to Narvik, confined to their cabins, they were put on a train to Rome. In this train they were allotted compartments with all the blinds drawn so they could not see or be seen by the crowds that had gathered at every station. The Fascist Party had put the machinery in place to humiliate Nobile and his crew and to have them branded as failures and cowards --- but the plan fell flat.

The expedition and rescue had caught the imagination of the Italian public as well as the world, and in spite of efforts to stop it, when Nobile and his crew arrived back in Rome on 31 July they were met by two hundred thousand cheering Italians; this wrecked Mussolini's plans for their humiliation. He had been hoping that his propagandists would have created a scenario blaming the failure of the expedition on Nobile's cowardice and incompetence---but it backfired.

The massive public backing gave Nobile the courage to go onto the attack. Not only did he condemn the incompetent back-up and involvement of the Italian authorities publicly, he did so to Mussolini's face. This was unwise. The Government held an official enquiry which allowed Nobile's detractors the oxygen of publicity with the result that the blame for the crash was put firmly at Nobile's door; he was also accused of abandoning his men in 'the red tent' on the ice -- charges that he would spend the next 20 years trying to overturn.

He was offered early retirement from his commission in the Italian Air Force with full pension rights but he was so furious that he resigned his commission forthwith and refused his pension.

Although it was becoming obvious that the future for aviation lay in aeroplanes rather than airships, he left Italy and went to help Russia with the design of their airships. When his wife died, he returned to Italy in 1936 to lecture on aeronautics at his alma mater, University of Naples, and on the outbreak of the Second World War he went to America to lecture in Lewis University in Illinois. He stayed in America until 1944 when Italy surrendered and when he returned he found a very changed Italy.

In 1945, an Italian Air Force tribunal cleared him of all charges related to the *Italia* crash and reinstated him to his former rank of Major General and restored his pension rights. He returned to lecture at Naples University where he stayed until he retired. He died in Rome on 30 July 1978 having seen the fiftieth anniversary of each of his Polar trips.

The age of airships ended in 1937 when the *Hindenberg* went on fire in full public view in New Jersey on 6 May killing 37 out of 95 passengers and crew. Showing the power that live media would have in the coming years, nothing did more for the demise of airships than the famous tearful radio commentary by Herbert Morrison.

'And after that,' said Maurizio, 'the Italians gave up the Arctic until we came on this boat'.

Chapter 19
Cheating

Don, Shirley and I, along with five of the Chinese, were sitting in a zodiac with a dud engine awaiting one of the logistics crew to come and repair it. Fortunately the sea was quite calm and our large yellow parkas were keeping us cosy, but situations like this always lead to a little anxiety . . . what if a whale turned us over or a polar bear came swimming towards us? Even the omnipotent Laurie might not have an answer.

But Shirley calmed us down by talking golf. She asked me if I'd ever had a hole in one. I said that I'd had one and several near misses.

'Were you alone or were you playing with a partner who could substantiate it?' she asked. I confirmed that I did have partners and that it was also memorable in another way. I was playing in a tournament at Deauville, France, on 6 June 1986, when I holed a 6 iron at the sixth hole using a Dunlop 65 golf ball with a number 6 on it.

'I've had one as well' said Shirley 'but I was playing on my own so I never reported it'.

'I'm sure that they would have believed you. You have such a truthful face. And, anyway, cheating at sport is a man-thing rather than a woman-thing'

'You don't know American women' she replied.

Golf at the North Pole

'I've got some insight into them' I replied 'because I'm a compulsive reader of the Decisions of the Rules of Golf Committee and I am always astonished at the number that seem to emanate from American women who must be *uber* competitive. My favourite query that the Rules committee had to resolve came from two American women who disagreed about the procedure when one lady was faced with playing her ball in a bunker while it was lying against a rattlesnake'

'I get it' said Shirley ' you can remove an impediment from a bunker but not an obstacle'

'Precisely' I replied. 'I'm not sure what happened but I think the opponent said the player had to play her ball, while she stood nearby ready to hit the rattlesnake with an iron club should it wake up'

'Know the type' said Shirley, 'but what's this Decisions book?'

'The Rules of Golf Committee meets four times a year and deals with questions about specific instances that come in from all over the world and provided the situation is not obviously covered in the Rules. These decisions are published every two years in a 700+ page book called (rather unimaginatively) *The Decisions of the Rules of Golf Committee'*.

I told her the story of the first set of rules ever written in 1744 by a Scottish surgeon called John Rattray.

The date is crucial to this story because at that time Scotland was still divided as to whether the Act of Union of 1707 joining it to England was a good or a bad thing. The arrival of Bonnie Prince Charlie in 1745 certainly polarised opinion and Rattray joined him as his personal physician when the campaign for the re-establishment of Scottish Independence started. As we know, that all ended in tears at the Battle of Culloden, when Bonnie Prince Charlie's army was annihilated. Rattray was captured and while he was standing in line in an Inverness churchyard waiting to be shot he was 'rescued' by his foursomes partner at Muirfield, the Hanoverian Lord Advocate, Duncan Forbes.

Rattray wrote 13 rules for the 'playing of the golf' and in the quarter of a millennium that has since passed, the number of rules has only just more than doubled. When you consider the huge change in golf course design, in the composition of the balls and clubs, and the professionalisation of the game, it becomes even more remarkable that today there are only 28 rules that govern the game worldwide. Yes, these 28 rules have subsections, but they, in themselves, are largely common sense and dictate that any given situation should be decided on 'fairness' (in the Book of Rules, the word used is 'equity').

Golf, unlike most other sports, has never been sullied by a cheating scandal. The world knows how Ben Johnson's rivalry with Carl Lewis played out with his 'win' in the 1988 Seoul Olympics and even more remarkably Lance Armstrong's evasion of a positive drug test until he had put seven Tour de France wins under his belt. Betting has made boxing a sporting laughing stock, and it is now contaminating even cricket and soccer.

Golf at the North Pole

Apart from James Bond's golf match with Goldfinger, which introduced most golfers to a world of cheating with which few were familiar, no one expects to play against a cheat.

Golf is probably unique among sports in that cheating is regarded as complete anathema to the participants and is actually very rare. Part of the valued tradition of golf is that you play by the rules and if you transgress one of those rules when no one sees you, it is expected that you will be your own referee and call a penalty on yourself.

Cheating in club golf is of course commoner than in professional golf, but the social penalties are just as great. If someone is caught cheating, their reputation is destroyed and they will for ever more have that stain on their character. However, most 'cheating' at this level comes from ignorance of the rules.

To be caught cheating in a professional golf event is tantamount to committing professional suicide; the PGA run a 'one strike and you're out' policy, so anyone caught cheating will be either expelled or suspended from their particular Tour.

Former Ryder Cup captain Colin Montgomery was playing in Singapore when the round was suspended because of a thunderstorm. Most golfers marked the position of their ball before leaving the course, but Montgomery left his ball where it had landed, a place that had a bunker between him and the green. When they went back the next day, his ball had disappeared and he replaced another ball in a position that took the bunker out of play. After an ensuing embarrassing row he gave his prize money to charity. There was no penalty on him because the referee was not satisfied that there had been 'intent' to cheat - and it was considered unlikely that a golfer of Montgomery's excellence would be put off by a bunker. It did however prove very damaging to his reputation.

We were still discussing the art of cheating when Bill (logistics) arrived in another zodiac, which he tied onto our boat and pulled us back to the ship before anything bad happened. All that we missed was an hour of walrus watching.

As we disembarked, Shirley said 'All this started because I told you I didn't report a hole in one when I was playing on my own. What's that got to do with where we're at now?'

'Lots,' I said. 'Follow me.'

I walked them through the lounge to the library, where the now 24/7 poker school was established. I asked Don if he thought any of the players were cheating. He said he didn't know because he didn't know how to cheat at poker.

'Some of the regular players can deal the second or third card - dealing from the bottom is one of the earliest things you learn when you get into card magic,' I said. 'Of course at least one, or more likely a pair here, are cheating.'

All the talk of cheating and bobbing about in a zodiac in the frozen sea cast my mind back to the story of Rear Admiral Byrd, whom Don had previously spoken about. Don had been a Navy pilot and was once shown documents prepared in 1958 by the Norwegian scientist,

Golf at the North Pole

explorer and aviator Bernt Balchen which were based on Byrd's logs and calculations, and which threw grave doubts on Byrd's claim to have been the first man to fly over both Poles.

Byrd's plane, a Fokker F-VII tri-motor, had taken him right across Antarctica, so he had definitely flown over the South Pole; therefore, when he claimed to have flown over the North Pole (just three days before Amundsen and Nobile had taken the *Norge* there) he was hailed as a hero -- and was of course believed.

Balchen's documents however showed that the plane had such a low top speed that it was unlikely that Byrd could have covered the distance he claimed in the time he recorded. He augmented that criticism in 1971 and went as far as to say that Byrd had merely circled aimlessly while out of sight of Spitsbergen from where he had taken off and returned at a time he reckoned people would believe that it had taken him to get to the Pole and back.

When Byrd returned to America in 1926, he produced a typewritten report for the National Geographic Society which managed to persuade them at least that he had accomplished what he had claimed, but the original diary and log never came to light until almost forty years after his death in 1996. These notes revealed erased (but still legible) sextant sights that sharply differed from his typewritten report.

Dennis Rawlins, the author who wrote about the lately discovered diaries, reckoned that Byrd flew about 80% of the way to the Pole and then turned back because of an engine oil leak.

He'd flown solo, so, rather like Shirley's hole in one, he had no corroboration -- after all, would a Rear Admiral lie?

By this time Klaus had joined in our conversation in the library. He agreed that massive deceptions can be created, asking had Man ever really reached the moon? Was the whole thing not just staged in the New Mexico desert?

'But your colleagues have to be trusted. How long could they keep up the deception?' I said. 'Richard Nixon said only two people could keep a secret -- provided one was dead'.

But Don, who'd been in New York on 9/11, challenged that. 'There were 13 terrorists involved in that plot. They'd known about it for months. They'd gone away to train. They'd lived apparently normal lives. And yet none of them gave a clue as to what they intended'.

'Of course they all died, so we will never know if all 13 could have stayed 'schtuum' for ever. That would be the problem if a group of you colluded to fraudulently fill in navigation logs while sitting in a tent, warm and safe, on an ice floe'.

I suggested that two of the most famous polar explorers had told probably lied about being the first to the North Pole, but my assertion was challenged by the other three.

'These men were not terrorists,' said Klaus. 'One of them would at some time in the future have spilled the beans'.

They refused to believe that a group could travel, not achieve their objective and then all collude to tell a whopping lie.

But I responded that if you went on your own, or with other men who don't fully understand what you were doing, then it would be quite possible that in all good faith they would back up their leader.

By and large at the beginning of the century, explorers took as few people as possible with them for the final push to the Pole because of the need for speed and minimal supplies. Nowadays it's possible to travel with a reasonably big group because technology has changed dramatically and although never an easy feat, it's a lot easier than it was at the beginning of the twentieth century when Peary and Cook, both of whom claimed to have been the first man on the North Pole, went on their trek.

Both of them were quite correct in surmising that with fewer people in the party there was less to go wrong and the fewer supplies they would have to carry . But also - and in retrospect, very importantly - the fewer witnesses there would be to confirm or deny their claim of success.

Both Peary and Cook travelled with Inuit help and Peary took his long-time manservant, the African-American Matthew Henson with him. Taking readings to confirm a position without GPS was a relatively complex task and it usually involved the leader making the readings, doing the calculations and calling them out to a colleague who would merely act as a scribe. It would usually only be the leader who was literate enough to be capable of writing up a log and a diary. And so, if they wanted, it was easy to cheat.

I then brought up the subject of the Rules for our tournament. We were of course going to have to write what are called Local Rules, which is normal practice when a tournament is to be played on any course. This is because there will be places on the course that might lead to a competitor feeling disadvantaged and in order to prevent referees being overworked or, more importantly, challenged, the Championship Committee must write a series of explanations as to procedure when a piece of local geography makes one of the 28 Rules difficult to interpret.

Since I seemed to know more about cheating than the others, it was agreed that I write the local rules that would govern our tournament.

Chapter 20
The Peary-Cook Controversy

Before I launch into the story of the two men, Robert Peary and Frederick Cook, who fought out a bitter dispute about who got to the North Pole first, I have to digress to talk about face-lifts.

There were 35 Americans on board, 20 women and 15 men. Of the 20 women, 12 had evidence of having had a face lift. I'm sure that each and every one of them would have been delighted at the outcome but to someone who knew about the procedure small imperfections are easy to spot.

I retired before the newer method of face lifting became established. The operation I could offer involved an enormous (hopefully invisible) incision within the hair line, undercutting skin to near the middle of the face, pulling on the skin, cutting off the excess and sewing it all up again. All of this took 3-4 hours and since skin is dynamic tissue, it started shrinking again almost immediately after the operation and the long term results were generally not worth either the surgeon's time or the patients' investment in self improvement.

The newer method is much better, involving only one or two small out of sight incisions, very little undercutting and pulling the face back by stitching the muscle under the skin to the mastoid bone behind the ear. This pulls the skin back far more naturally but errors can still be made; a stitch can be too superficial, a stitch may come out, the tension here and there can be too great, but basically I'm not a fan of the procedure because I think that someone in their eighth decade should not look like someone in their thirties!

The reason I digress into face lifts is that the lady from Chicago who had led us into the Cook-Peary story had had a pretty good face lift but by the 5th day I'd counted 3 imperfections. Her name was Rosemary and she had known the late Janet Vetters, the granddaughter of Frederick Cook.

Janet Vetters was a very faithful loving granddaughter who went to her grave believing passionately that her grandfather had been unjustly treated by the US 'establishment'.

To ensure that the fight to restore his reputation was continued, when she died in 1989, she left a tax exempt educational trust of a million dollars (producing $91,000 per annum tax free) for any researchers who could write positively in favour of her grandfather.

Rosemary had no doubt that Ms Vetters was correct and that Peary was a dreadful man who had 'done down' the perfectly respectable and honest Frederick Cook. On the other hand, Bob, an American former newspaperman and now a philanthropist, held the view that Cook was a con-man and that although Peary might not have reached exactly 90 degrees north he had near as dammit reached the Pole.

Great! Another tournament, this time to search for the truth. The playing field was decided as were the rules of engagement. The discussion was to begin over happy hour, continue through dinner and be finally fought out over that evening's vodka cocktails.

We met at six and I asked Rosemary to kick off by telling us her impression of Peary's personality. Bob could challenge after she had finished but was not allowed to interrupt.

She started by saying that Peary was rather odd, a thing that Bob did not disagree with. I asked her if there were any early reasons for this.

'Peary had been a 'mummy's boy' ever since his father died when he was very young. He clung to his mother and his mother clung to him and he spent the rest of his life trying to make his mother proud of him.

She wouldn't let him play with other children in case they intervened in the role modeling she had planned for him and like many Victorian mothers they felt that nature study was a good prophylactic against any thoughts about sex'

She went on. 'He was intelligent enough to graduate from High School and get a College placement, as well as a scholarship. But while most boys who go to College leave home and come back at vacation times, this wasn't what Mrs Peary had in mind for her little boy. When he went to Bowdion College in Brunswick, Maine to study engineering, she went as well and even stayed with him until he graduated as a civil engineer.

Usually, a son who has graduated with a professional qualification might be expected to go out into the world to find a job, but once again, his mother had different ideas. She was not having her precious son disappearing off to some place where she had no control over him and so she arranged that they both go and live in a tiny hamlet in Maine--- where there was absolutely nothing to do'.

'What happened next was freaky' said Rosemary, 'He joined the Navy'

'I've no idea how he managed to leave home but he did and he didn't like it. Instead of being put on a boat and sent to faraway places he was stuck in a surveyors office which was not what he had in mind. He stuck it for a little while and then resigned -- for a reason that would resonate with the young today-- he wanted to be famous. In his own words ---"I wanted to acquire a name which shall make my mother proud".

'After failing to find work as an engineer in civilian life he re-joined the Navy.' continued Rosemary. 'This time the posting was more to his taste; he was sent to survey Nicaragua, which, at the time, was being considered as an alternative site for a canal through Central America. Panama was finally chosen as the preferred site but while working in hot sticky Nicaragua he acquired a fascination for the wilderness. He did a lot of reading during those long sweaty days but his favourite reading was about the exact opposite -- the cold places. One of the books that he was particularly fond of was Nordenskiold's description of his failed expedition to cross Greenland on skis'.

'On his first leave after the spell in Nicaragua, he borrowed $500 from his mother, bought a berth on a sealer to Greenland and when they landed he set out on skis to explore what was then an icy wilderness. He claimed to have gone 100 miles inland--- but this claim was later seriously challenged by no less a critic than Nansen'

Then came Rosemary's first barb 'I wonder if this wasn't his first attempt at telling 'Porkies' to see if he could get away with it or whether he was a useless navigator?'

'Absolutely rubbish' spluttered Bob, who had done well to maintain his continence during the preceding 'hatchet job'.

'OK, you're turn Bob, tell us what a paragon of virtue Cook was"

'I don't know if you become a con-man through your genes or your environment but my money is on Cook having con-man genes' he started.

'He was 'bent' right from the start, but he, like all these guys, was clever. He was never bombastic and his constant modest manner made him more credible. Was he just accident-prone and misunderstood. No, I don't think anyone could create a record like his if it was just chance'

'Listen' Bob said ' this is a guy who claimed to have written a dictionary of an ancient South American tribal language when he had actually stolen it from an old scholar in Chile. He falsely claimed to have climbed one of the highest peaks in America, and then tried to con the world into believing that he'd reached the North Pole. When they put him in the slammer for 14 years for stock fraud, they finally caught up with him and he got what was coming to him.'

I reminded Bob that Rosemary had given a credible reason for Peary's personality. So I asked him if there was anything similar in Cook's background.

'His father had emigrated from Germany in 1848 and like over 30,000 other native-born Germans living in New York, he fought with the Union Army in the Civil War, and in those days that was a big plus for any immigrant because it meant that he and his family would have become true Americans and would be accepted into American mainstream society'.

'After the war the father took his family to the Catskill mountain area of upstate New York where he opened a medical practice that flourished. However when Frederick was only 5, his father died, leaving the family with no income. Frederick does seem to have had a great childhood, delighting in finding his way about the wilderness of the mountains and also learning to rock climb. He certainly wasn't a 'mummy's boy' and seemed very self sufficient when he left home.

'He went to medical school in Brooklyn to do a short 2 year course-- and how you become a doctor in only two years even then beats me' said Bob. 'The poor guy married before he finished his course but his wife died in childbirth the day he got his results, so you have to feel sorry for him'.

'He opened a medical practice, but not surprisingly, could not settle and that might have been because he didn't learn many 'cures' in his 2 year course!

Golf at the North Pole

'Foul' shouted Rosemary, but I asked Bob to carry on.

'He met up with Robert Peary as a result of answering a newspaper advert for the post of a surgeon-physician to accompany an expedition that Robert Peary was planning to Greenland. Cook must have been desperate to get away from New York because he happily closed his practice and signed up for the trip for the paltry sum of $50.

To be fair to him he was probably so desperate to do something other than medicine in New York that he subsequently admitted that he didn't pay much attention to the small print of the contract and so he missed the bit preventing him from publishing anything about the expedition until Robert Peary granted permission. When he later wanted to break this condition he fell out with Peary because the latter refused him permission to publish a medical article because it did relate to the expedition'.

Klaus had been listening and found it hard to believe that something as small as this broke up a friendship. We then explained to him the fact was that in the early pre-media days the way to make money after an expedition was to write a book and go on a lecture tour charging large admission fees. There was no television and no films so the lecture circuit could be very profitable to good presenters especially if they had been to exotic places and had lanternslides.

I said 'OK, we've got them together for their first expedition. Did they get on well? Was Cook of any help to Peary? What happened?'

I gave the floor to Rosemary for the next bit.

'They sailed out of New York on the old barkentine *SS Kite* in June 1891 and apart from the ship's crew there was a gaggle of others on board. Altogether there were 9 scientists of which two came to a sticky end, both blaming Peary. Elvin Astrup, was taken along because he was a good skier, hunter and climber. Gregor Verhoef was taken not only because he would be useful as a geologist but he had been so keen to go that he paid Peary $2000 for a berth'.

A month after they sailed, Peary slipped on the deck and fractured his lower leg. Cook set it but legs take a long time to heal and when they reached Greenland two weeks later Peary had to be carried ashore on planks'.

'They had planned to 'winter' in a wooden house that they built from a model kit and they christened it Red Cliff House and persuaded some nomadic Inuits to move their encampment closer so that they could learn some of the language and also get some instruction on how to live in the hostile environment. The Inuits happily obliged because of the gifts of tools and weapons that they were given and they, in return, taught the Americans how to hunt, how to make and use sledges and how get used to eating uncooked meat'.

'But surely the most important thing they learned was how to dress and how useless woolens would be in that environment' I said. Rosemary and Bob agreed.

They spent the winter training for the spring expedition by experimenting with different methods of driving dogs, harnessing them, preparing skis and

Golf at the North Pole

building and loading sledges. In February when the weather began to improve Peary sent Cook and Astrup to break the trail and lay down supplies and in April, he and Henson, his African-American manservant, followed them. The latter pair were thus able to move more quickly because of the work that Cook had done and when they caught up with the advance party in June, they sent Cook and Astrup back to base'

'Peary was on a tight timetable because the *SS Kite* was coming back for them in late July and the ship had to get back out into open water before the ice started to form in August; if they were caught in the ice the ship would be damaged and they might be stranded. Peary managed to get back by the skin of his teeth but then there occurred an episode that might shine a light on Peary's personality as a leader and commander'.

'The geologist, Gregor Verhoef did not travel back with them because he said that he had vowed never again to associate with Peary or never ever to go on a ship with him. He is reported to have gone off exploring on his own but was never seen again. The fact that the others left without him might also say something about Verhoef's state of mind and personality.'

'Although that expedition did not achieve very much they were met by enthusiastic crowds when the ship berthed in New York and that enthused them for more Arctic exploration but then came the spat about publication. Cook must have been more put out than Peary because when Peary invited him to go on the next expedition, Cook refused'.

'But the sting in the tail of that Greenland expedition came when Eivind Astrup, the expert skier and the man who had broken the trail with Cook, committed suicide, citing Peary's treatment of him as the cause of his depression'

'OK, I'll go along with all of that' said Bob.

Over dinner I thought I should take over and summarise the middle bit of the story to leave the two protagonists fresh for the final debate.

Cook then went into the Arctic cruise business. He hired a boat called the *Miranda* and took 50 rich passengers at $500 each to visit the north of Greenland. The trip was a disaster that put this fledgling career to the sword.

Among other things, the captain was a drunk and they were nearly wrecked while trying to berth at Sukkertoppen (Maniitsoq), a town on the west coast of Greenland. Cook had arranged for the passengers to have some land excursions that they all enjoyed and things were coming together nicely until the drunken captain again hit a reef on the way out of harbour.

Although the captain wanted to go on, Cook insisted that they returned to harbour in order to commission another ship to tow the *Miranda* home, a decision which was vindicated when, while in tow, the *Miranda* sank and all the passengers had to be transferred to the tow ship, the *Rigel*. When this reached Nova Scotia the paying passengers, not surprisingly, decided that they had had enough and all disembarked in order to get trains to their homes; that was the end of Cook's Cruises.

After this debacle Cook reluctantly went back to medical practice but when the opportunity came to go with a Belgian expedition to the Antarctic he accepted. This was an important milestone in his exploring experiences because Roald Amundsen was the first mate on the ship and they got on very well. They were iced up over the winter and it was not until early 1899 that they managed to dig a lead and sail out of their icy prison. Over the winter there had been many medical problems with the crew and Cook's efforts were greatly appreciated, especially by Amundsen.

Bob interrupted. 'That really has nothingto do with the 'big con' that Cook attempted'

Rosemary replied 'And who was paying for Peary all this while? Wasn't he supposed to be a low ranking naval officer who managed to con people, just like Cook, only this time so that he could be a paid 'amateur' explorer?. During every expedition for which he had had leave he was drawing pay from the Navy and doing absolutely nothing for it.

He was beginning to think of the Arctic as his own domain and thus an American dependence. He felt justified by this and felt that the Navy should go along with this 'patriotism' and pay him to 'play'. He tried to use this 'threat to American domination of the Arctic' to get another expedition mounted, but this time the Navy said 'No'. This was not surprising since this most recent request was for five years leave of absence -- with full pay! By this point in his Naval career, he had been in service for 8 years and 5 months and of that time he had been on leave with pay for 7 years and 1 month'

'But with all his contacts that were to prove useful later they got President McKinlay to intervene and he was granted the leave that he wanted--- with full pay!'

'Nor was he totally celibate during these periods of absence. It transpired that both he and Henson had sired children with Inuit women whom they had 'shared' with other Inuit men.

When his wife Josephine found out and expressed displeasure, he argued that it was useful to humanity that another race be developed 'with white man's brains and Inuit hardiness'! This guy was in another world' Rosemary continued.

Peary made his first Polar attempt sailing with the *Windward* at the age of 42 in 1898, but he had to give up only 343 miles from the Pole. He was under the impression that he had at least created a new 'furthest north' record. But disappointment awaited him. The Italian, Captain Umberto Cagni, a second in command of the expedition led by the Duke of Abruzzi (Chapter 17), had reached 137 miles further.

During this abortive attempt Peary had shown amazing determination because he had continued to press on in the vilest of conditions, despite frostbite that was so severe that when he got back to base he carried out his own amputations merely by snapping off his toes one by one. He was able to do this because his devitalised tissue had luckily not become infected and he was suffering from so-called 'dry' gangrene.

Before Peary returned to the Arctic in 1902, he got the surgeon who had secretly operated on President

Cleveland's maxillary sinus tumour, to perform plastic surgery on his feet so that the area where the toes used to be was at least covered by skin. This meant that from that point on Peary would only have the use of his feet as stumps and would have no 'spring' in his step.

He went back on duty with the Navy but was soon busy trying to raise money for yet another attempt on the Pole, this time using a boat that would get nearer to the Pole by breaking further through the ice thus lessening the distance that he would have to walk. The problem was that this design would be much more expensive than the usual Arctic ship and the cost could rise to six figures-- a huge sum a hundred years ago.

When President McKinlay was assassinated, he was succeeded by a sportsman and adventurer, Theodore Roosevelt, who was totally in tune with this naval officer with a sense of adventure and a fierce patriotism. Roosevelt was instrumental in getting the funding so that the new ship could be constructed and so it was therefore appropriate that it was named the *Roosevelt*.

Peary departed on 16 July 1905 and the ship did what it was meant to do; it got 300 miles closer to the Pole than any other ship had ever done before, so that when Peary set off trekking in March, he calculated that he could get to the Pole in 100 days using the techniques of travel and clothing he had learned over the years from the Inuit.

One of the basic strategies was to get advance teams to lay down supply depots at regular intervals and to break out a route, then the main team could march with virtually no unnecessary stops and with less load on their

,ledges. But the advance party that year did not move as quickly as had been hoped for because of the size of the ice hummocks and also the breadth of the leads. When it became obvious that he was not going to be successful in reaching the Pole, he gave up on the primary aim and went for the 'furthest north' record.

He claimed to have done this. But the problem was, that even though he had kept meticulous records on all of his previous trips, he made no notes or calculations during the last three days on this one, a period in which, were he to have achieved the record, he would have had to cover 90 miles; in other words an almost unbelievable 30 miles a day. This was stretching credibility too far because in similar circumstances, Nansen had travelled only 7 miles a day and Cagni, nine.

He must have been in the mood to deceive because when he got back to the ship he did some local exploring and claimed to have discovered new islands--- but he hadn't. All he had done was to mistakenly 'discover' already discovered islands in the archipelago and rename them in honour of some of his sponsors who were subsequently embarrassed. One of the more embarrassing examples was naming a piece of land as Jessup Land (after his sponsor Morris Jessup) not realising that that particular rock had already been christened Axel Heiberg Land by Otto Sverdrup in 1901 after one of his sponsors. He was fortunate that this gross error or deliberate deception was not later dredged up in the fight that was to follow with Cook.

At this point Bob interrupted and asked if he could continue by telling Cook's mountaineering story.

Golf at the North Pole

I said 'OK but it's got to be fair'

'While Peary was gaining all this far north experience, Cook had once again opened a medical practice and married a wealthy young widow with a daughter whom he adopted. But as usual, he got bored and he was off again, this time mountaineering. He went exploring around Mount McKinlay in Alaska and said he had circumnavigated the range walking 700 and boating 300 miles.

He made another attempt on the mountain the next year and claimed to have climbed to the summit with a porter called Edward Barille. They were away for only a month and Cook announced that they had hit upon a totally unknown route and had reached the summit on 16 September 1906. This got him elected President of the Explorers Club of New York and the financial backing of a millionaire sportsman, John R Bradley, for further expeditions.

'Another hole in one while playing on your own' interrupted Shirley caustically.

'Don't worry Bob' I said 'tell us about Bradley'

'John R Bradley had become rich through betting. He had a gambling club in Palm Beach and his offer to finance Cook for a North Pole attempt was contingent upon Cook taking him to the Arctic so that he could hunt. Cook had a custom designed boat built, christened her the *John R Bradley,* and left New York in July 1907 with supplies for at least two years. As they were leaving, Cook informed the various interested organisations, among which was the newly formed Peary Arctic Club, that he was intending to find a new route to the North Pole. Peary, who regarded the North Pole as 'his own', was incensed, but he received the information too late for him to do anything about it other than plan a chase'.

'John Bradley was happy to stay in the Arctic a couple of months, slaughter anything that moved and then return to New York in the ship, along with his huge haul of polar bear and walrus trophies, leaving Cook to prepare for his attempt for the Pole'.

'In February 1908, at the first sign of the sun, Cook, a German scientist Rudolph Franke, nine Inuits and 103 dogs set off to create a base for a polar attempt. They chose as their base a well constructed hut on Cape Sabine, Ellesmere Island that had been preserved from the previous American Army expedition led by the unlucky Captain Greely (Chapter 10). There, Cook claimed to have left his collection of blue fox furs, narwhal horns and walrus ivory that he had evidently acquired through trading with the Inuit, in the care of the Rudolph Franke with instructions to ship the collection back to America if he hadn't returned by July.

Meanwhile, President Roosevelt told the Navy to give Peary another three year fully paid leave of absence enabling him to sail out of New York on 6 July 1908 with the ship captained by Robert Bartlett. They arrived at the Inuit settlement of Etah in south Greenland in August where they were joined by another party of sportsmen and hunters in a ship chartered by the Peary Club of New York called *Erik*. Among the hunters travelling on that ship was a 34 year old man from Connecticut, Harry

Whitney, who was to be dragged unwillingly into the upcoming fight between Peary and Cook.'

At this point I interrupted and said 'We're coming to a difficult bit now and it might be better if I took over to avoid a shouting match'

'This was to be Peary's last chance to get to the Pole and do something that would make him everlastingly famous, a drive had been with him ever since his father had died. He was now 53 which was old for Arctic exploration, but he was a driven man in spite of his limp from the old lower limb fracture and the fact that he had no toes.

His mood however was far worse than his physical state and when he arrived at Cape Sabine and found Franke in pretty poor shape, wanting to go home and begging for help, the story goes that Peary would not even give him a cup of coffee since he was 'tainted' by association with Cook. Peary only allowed him on board with a promise of a berth home if he signed over all Cook's possessions to him.

'Lies' said Bob.

Ignoring this expected interruption I continued.

'Peary left his boatswain in charge of the house and put a notice on the door of the store-house which said

"This house belongs to Dr F A Cook but he is long since dead and there is no use to search for him. I, Commander Robert E Peary, install my boatswain in this deserted house"

If that was showing ill feeling on Peary's part, there was much worse to come!

Then there's a big blank in the story where both men seemed to have disappeared.

'We know little about Cook's journey to the North Pole apart from the fact that he reduced his final party to two young Inuits, Etukishook and Ahweiah, 2 sledges, 26 dogs and food for 48 days before starting the 580 mile march to the Pole.

He then, like Nansen, disappeared from the world, until, after 14 months he arrived back in Anoatok, a village near the larger Inuit settlement of Etah, Greenland in April 1909.

Although Peary was well behind Cook when they started out he did a fairly quick return journey and so arrived back in civilisation shortly after Cook.

Then both men behaved very oddly. Neither came bounding in waving his arms in the air saying 'Yippee' I've reached the North Pole and I got back!'

At this point Don, who had been quietly listening to the debate butted in,

'If I'd reached the North Pole I would have been whooping with delight, and if the clothes allowed me, I'd be doing backward somersaults' he said. 'I know that "cool" is fashionable nowadays but to say nothing after you'd become the first man to reach the top of the world is at best, odd, especially if that is what you'd spent your life attempting'

I thought that I'd better continue the story once again since tempers were rising.

Golf at the North Pole

'Cook met the American hunter Harry Whitney and told him about his long absence, but initially nothing about reaching the North Pole. When Peary got back to the *Roosevelt* he did not tell the crew he had reached the Pole nor did he mention it to Bartlett with whom he had been so close'.

'Cook was the first to make the claim and he did so only after hearing from Harry Whitney about Peary's treatment of Franke , the purloining all his goods from Cape Sabine and the premature announcement of his death. He said he'd reached the Pole on April 21 1908, a year before Peary. When asked later why he hadn't said anything earlier his excuse was that he was still suffering from the stress that he and his two young Inuit colleagues had suffered in their fight for survival on the return journey'

'He said that they'd arrived at the Pole after a tough journey but that was nothing compared to what they had to face on the return leg. He said that when they got to the Pole he had left a note in a brass tube.

The return journey had then been a nightmare because of the ice floe drift. They had been taken east of Axel Heiberg Island (which is to the west of Ellesmere Island). The drift continued and by the September, as winter was closing in they had reached the north cape of Devon island which lies south east of Ellesmere and is well inside the Canadian Arctic but still not a place that one would wish to stay during a winter.

There they found an ice cave which they dug out, finding a human skull in the process, and lived by hunting musk ox which let them survive from

November to February at which time they had started on the homeward march to Etah which had taken two months'.

'Peary was more explicit about his trip, but like Cook was a bit vague about the actual last bit of getting to the Pole. He had sent off advance parties to break a way through hummocks and to lay down stores. He himself travelled with Matthew Henson, Robert Bartlett, and 4 other crew members and scientists along with 11 sledges and 14 Inuit drivers.'

'On 30 March he sent Bartlett's group back, much to the latter's dismay, since he desperately wanted to be in the party who got to the Pole. This left Peary with Henson and 4 Inuit and at that point they were 134 miles from the Pole having averaged only 13 miles a day for the previous month. At that rate it was going to take him another 10 days to reach the Pole and perhaps a couple of days less to return to that point'.

Peary claimed to have arrived within 5 miles of the Pole on 6 April 1909 and set up what he called 'Camp Jessup' . Along with him were Henson, Ootah, Egigingwah, Seegloo and Ooqueah none of whom were capable of taking navigation readings.

When Peary heard of Cook's claim he went ballistic, called him a liar and said the only people who had been to the Pole were himself, Matthew Henson and the 4 Inuits!

Bob grudgingly agreed that all of this was rather odd but he 'rubbished' Cook's story about losing all his documents. He continued; 'According to Cook the con-

Golf at the North Pole

man, Whitney wanted him to wait for the boat that would take them both back to America, but Cook said that he wanted to announce his success at being the first to arrive at the Pole in Denmark, and that was where he aimed to go. He then marched South without most of his papers that could have verified his claims. I just don't believe his story of Whitney's offer to see that all his personal items were taken back to America. And furthermore I just find it incredible that Cook packed three boxes for Whitney containing all his instruments and half of the record of his journey, keeping in his possession only the manuscript of his diary, some field papers and some sextant readings. Why did he ask Whitney and his friends not to say anything about his claim to have reached the Pole to Peary or anyone else, and why did he give the same instructions to his original Inuit companions, Etukishook and Ahweiah'.

I took up the rest of the story.

Cook reached Upernavik in northwestern Greenland and stayed with the Danish Governor until there was a ship going back to Copenhagen in August. During that trip to Denmark he gave many lectures about his successful polar journey, and when he arrived in the Shetland Isles, he telegraphed both his wife and Whitney's mother. He also then telegraphed the *New York Herald,* one of his sponsors, to announce the fact that he had conquered the Pole a year before Peary.

As they docked in Copenhagen the ship was invaded by journalists from all over the world, one of whom, Philip Gibbs of the *London Daily Chronicle,* asked to see his diaries. Cook replied that he had left them at his

Greenland base and so Gibbs did the unforgiveable for a reporter at the start of the twentieth century---he posed an impertinent question to an emerging hero;

"What evidence can you bring to show you actually reached the Pole ? "

Shirley butted in; 'As much evidence as I have for my hole in one'

Cook was received by King Frederick of Denmark and when he went to his Hotel, The Phoenix, there were more than 50 reporters waiting to quiz him. He was asked if he had actually set foot on the North Pole and he replied honestly "I doubt if anybody could do that. I think I got within the circle and went round it for two days making observations'

He was then asked " What does it look like?"

"Ice" he replied.

He turned down a huge offer from the Hearst newspaper group for his story in favour of a $25,000 offer from the *New York Herald* which had supported him. But doubts were raised right away when articles by Philip Gibbs started appearing in the *New York Tribune*, the paper that had supported Peary. While he was at a farewell dinner hosted by the Royal Danish Geographic Society, a telegram arrived for the *New York Tribune* representative, a Mr Stead.

It said *"Stars and Stripes nailed to the North Pole. Peary"*

Unfazed, Cooke gave a short speech warmly praising Peary's success and he asked the *Tribune* to send his congratulations to Peary.

Golf at the North Pole

But that is when the trouble really began. Peary, from Labrador, wired the Associated Press.

"Cook's story should not be taken too seriously. The two Eskimos (sic) who accompanied him say he went no distance North and not out of sight of land".

Chapter 21
The Aftermath

By now we'd collected quite an audience because although almost all of them had heard of the Cook-Peary controversy no one was very clear about the details of the story. As we'd been going over the personalities of the two men at dinner some people had come to listen in and by the time we retreated to the bar we'd collected an audience of 8 or 9 people and we were all seated round one of the tables in the bar wondering if it would be in the interests of our health to have a dry evening. Klaus excluded himself from such talk.

I started the discussion by saying 'In my opinion neither of them reached the North Pole but Peary had more powerful friends and he himself was far more media savvy than Cook'.

That did not go down well with Bob and several of the others.

'OK' he said 'we know that Cook faked it but why should Peary?'

I said to him 'He was 53, he had no chance of getting more time off from the Navy, Roosevelt or no Roosevelt, and so he wasn't going back. If someone like Peary had actually been to the North Pole he would have returned to the ship with drums banging, trumpets playing and flags waving. OK, I know that instruments might not have been readily available but surely to God he would have told the first person he met and at least Bartlett his Captain who was so disappointed to have been sent back. And ask yourself this, why did he send him back if he didn't want to be the only one to do the navigation?'

'When did he make the announcement? Right after he heard Cook's claim. You can imagine what he must have felt like. Here he was the world expert in Arctic exploration, Arctic weather, ice conditions and survival technique; no one knew more, even the great Nansen, and on top of that he was a patriot and felt he was doing this for America. Then along comes Cook and 'gazumps' him with not very much evidence that he was telling the truth either.'

Bob butted in and said ' With his expertise and experience, he knew for certain that Cook could not possibly have reached the Pole; he knew there was no 'new route' west of Ellesmere Island and he doubted Cook's ability to navigate and survive at the limit.

He knew Cook better than most, having travelled with him, and if he deemed that Cook was capable of a deception like this then he could well have been correct.'

'I agree with you that Peary was as much of a con man as Cook, but what makes you doubt that Cook made it?' Rosemary asked me.

'Same reason. If I'd got to the North Pole I'd tell the first person I met and would try to broadcast it far and wide. But although we know that Cook wasn't a showy sort of person he would at least have told Harry Whitney who seemed like a friend. But he didn't say anything about it until he heard how badly Peary had treated Franke and how he had virtually 'stolen' his possessions. What more natural than to skewer a man like that where it would hurt most?'

I added that I thought that Peary's response was more about his relationship with Cook than about a major world discovery, saying 'Peary went on the attack immediately he arrived in Greenland; the first thing he did was to fire off 17 telegrams. To the *New York Times,* which was one of his sponsors, he wrote; *"Don't let Cook story worry you. Have him nailed"* . 'Well he would wouldn't he. What he needed more than anything was to keep his sponsors on-side'

'A day later he sent *"Cook has simply handed the public a gold brick. He's not been to the Pole on April 21 1908 or at any other time"*. Why was he virtually repeating himself?. What were his thoughts when he woke up at 4am that day.?

When he arrived in Labrador he had arranged to be met by the worlds' reporters and he held court for a week.

'He had to be hiding something because he did not let the reporters talk to anyone except himself and some cabin boy' said Rosemary.

'Because only he and not the ships' crew had gone to the Pole' replied Bob. 'You're clutching at straws'

'Well what about the grilling he gave Cook's two Inuits, Ahwelah and Etukishook? He might have sired an Inuit son but that doesn't mean he could speak the language especially to probe difficult situations like this. This was the first piece of evidence he quoted in one of the first telegrams--"*The two Eskimos that accompanied him said they had travelled no distance north and not out of sight of land*". 'He got a lot of mileage out of that piece of news because his translation of what the lads said was that they had only been 15-20 miles away from land and had just wandered about. So how did Cook persuade two Inuit boys to stay on the ice, when they were not many miles from their families, for over a year, so that he could pull off a bluff? From Peary's translation of what the boys said it appeared that Cook had threatened to harm them and their families if they didn't back him up. So you're on the ice for over a year with two Inuit boys, you're all dependent on each other for survival, you live in a snow hole hunting musk ox for several months -- and you threaten them? A likely tale!' said Rosemary.

'Just like I said earlier' I chipped in. 'If you take along guys who don't know a longitude reading from a lollipop you could say anything you wanted'

Rosemary's next point was; 'Peary's next salvo was to question Cook's account of the time it took him to reach the Pole in his final push. He compared Cook's 15 miles a day with Cagni's 'best' of 7 miles, but when Cook responded by saying it was quite possible since Peary must have done 30 miles a day if his figures were correct, that argument went quiet'

'Well' said Bob 'it was Cook's own fault. If he'd produced fuller records with all of his readings then he would have been in a position to prove the distances he'd claimed but what did he do? He put them all in a box, left it with Harry Whitney whom he didn't know from Adam, asking him to take the records back to America. Why didn't he take them himself since he decided to announce his discovery in Copenhagen rather than America. I'll tell you why. He planned a win-win situation for himself. If the box didn't come back he could blame either Whitney or Peary, and if it did come back, he could argue that Peary must have gone through the records and redacted them. That sort of thinking comes easy to a con-man'

I continued the story by telling them how the end-game was played out.

'Up till that point it had just been a playground squabble-- 'you did, you didn't' etc. Then it got nasty.'

'Peary had powerful friends with loads of money right up to Presidential level. Out of the blue his side produced Edward Barille, the man who'd gone up Mount McKinlay with Cook. Barille said that Cook and he had colluded in a scam, taking photographs of 'the summit' when they were miles away. He said that Cook and he had not climbed higher than 8000 feet and were more than 20 miles from the summit'

Golf at the North Pole

'Cook was so astonished at this, or apparently so, that he took himself off to Montana, right across America, to confront Barille, but to his surprise he found out the reason that Barille had produced the sworn statement to Peary's friends.

The former blacksmith had now bought a five bedroom house with an orchard and was the first man in Montana to buy a car. It later transpired that his statement had been 'bought' for $250,000!'

'That was followed up by the University of Copenhagen getting cold feet at what they'd been led to believe and when Cook could not produce his papers they withdrew all the honours they had bestowed on him having been even more embarrassed since they had involved their King'.

'That was the knock out blow, and while Cook disappeared from the scene for a year, Peary was officially recognised as the discoverer of the North Pole both by Congress and the National Geographic Society. He was promoted to Rear Admiral and given an $8000 a year pension.

But as Peary basked in his glory for another decade his main feeling would be that his mother, looking down on him from heaven, would have been proud of him. And especially when he was buried in America's cemetery for heroes, Arlington'.

'Yes, he was a lucky man' said Rosemary. 'He was lucky no one in the National Geographic Society asked any questions when they reviewed his logs and diaries -- beautifully written on clean paper -- even though he hadn't washed in weeks and had been handling pemmican and greasy blubber every day!'. They were all made up'

She continued 'When you're down they keep kicking. Any other episode like this would have blown over and been replaced by another story but this was so big the Press kept digging and that's what really upset Janet Vettel and her mother'.

She said, 'When Cook reappeared from Europe in 1910, *Hampton's Magazine* had another go at him. They 'innocently' asked him to write his version of events for the magazine. He did so, but allowed the magazine to 'edit' it.

As we know, only 'new' stories 'sell' and so for *Hamptons* to publish a straight story about Cook reaching the North Pole would not have been 'new'. So they edited it, virtually re-writing it into an essay that they had hoped he would have written'.

'What came out was headlined as '*Cook's Confession*' in which he was quoted as saying that he was 'uncertain as to having reached the exact mathematical Pole". The confirmation of the 'big edit' and falsification came out years later from the typist who had prepared the 'new' material for the compositors. And I have to ask you Bob, if he was indeed a 'con-man' then he should have been one step ahead of anyone wanting to 'con' him, but from this episode in the sad story, that doesn't appear to have been the case'.

Rosemary continued 'Janet Vettel told me that in 1914, a US Senator, Miles Poindexter, received a letter from a member of an Arctic expedition saying that he had talked to the two Eskimos Ahwelah and Etukishook and they had corroborated the fact that 'they had gone very far from land for a very long time' which contradicted Peary's report of the interview. Poindexter arranged for another commission of enquiry but the onset of the First World War and Peary's influential political friends had it squashed.'

The story had a very sad end no matter whose side you're on.

Cook disappeared from East Coast society and went into oil prospecting in Wyoming, about as far away from Peary as he could get. When oil was discovered in Texas, he went south and formed the PPA (Petroleum Producers Association); this organisation sold stock to small companies who could not afford development but had valuable holdings.

In 1923 he was accused of a giant stock reloading scheme and after a five week trial he was sentenced to 15 years in the Leavenworth penitentiary, one of the worst in the country.

He was finally pardoned and released in 1930, penniless and in poor health. It was ironic that the land for which he was selling stock in 1922 which had only produced 245,000 barrels in the first two years, was now producing 32 million barrels a year.

He died ten years later from a stroke.

Unfortunately for him he didn't live long enough to see what some might call (Janet Vettel being one) his partial redemption.

A G D Maran

In 1985, the National Geographic Society commissioned the British explorer, Sir Wally Herbert, who had walked across the Arctic in 1968 and who at one time had been a great Peary admirer, to examine the papers to which the Peary family had granted unlimited access. They were forced into doing this in response to a 1984 TV programme called *Race for the Pole* that portrayed a naive Dr Cook being deprived of his just honour by a malevolent Peary.

Herbert's conclusions appeared in the September 1988 issue of the National Geographic Magazine, and his opinions were absolutely NOT what either the Peary Family or the National Geographic Society wanted to hear.

For a start, Herbert said that Peary's claim to a 'furthest north' in 1906 was impossible to accept because if it were true it meant that Peary had had to do a march of 77 miles in a day.

Herbert went on to conclude that it was impossible for Peary to have reached the Pole given the observations that he had made; furthermore it was unlikely that he had even come within a 100 miles of it.

Herbert rightly stated that in all cases, the burden of proof lies with the explorer, and in his opinion Peary had not supplied this. On the other hand, in his book T*he Noose of Laurels* he completely debunks the possibility that Cook was ever near the Pole either.

To defend their pro-Peary stance, the National Geographic Society asked a minor body called the *Navigation Foundation* to look at the evidence that Herbert had refuted, and they fortunately produced the answer that the National Geographic Society wanted, but it did not convince the experts on the other side.

Closely following this, a neuroscience professor at Harvard, S. Allen Counter, published a book in 1991, *North Pole Legacy; Black White and Eskimo*. Counter was a great supporter of the African-American Matthew Henson, Peary's constant servant and companion.

He interviewed the out-of-wedlock sons of both Peary and Henson, Anaukaq Henson and Kali Peary. In spite of attempts by the Peary family to block him, Counter managed to bring both boys to the United States in 1987. The following year Counter was able to have Henson's remains buried in Arlington next to Peary's grave with a designation, 'co-discoverer' of the North Pole

The argument goes on today, and in an attempt to test one of the main criticisms of Peary's claim, Tom Avery, a British explorer, led an expedition in 2005 to try to replicate Peary's time using the same type of wooden sledges and Inuit dog teams. They set out from the same starting point as Peary, Cape Columbia on Ellesmere Island, and covered the 765 kilometres to the Pole some four hours faster than Peary and Henson but the longest average distance travelled over the final 5 days was only 90 nautical miles a feat that had left six very fit young trained and experienced men exhausted. Peary, with a limp and no toes, had claimed a 135 miles per day average.

Although Avery in his book T*o the End of the Earth* concluded that Peary could have reached the Pole, many readers doubted his conclusion because he was comparing a more rugged landscape travelled by a man with no toes and a painful old fracture, to a milder landscape travelled by four young fit explorers.

Sir Wally Herbert was not a fan of the Avery expedition. He impugned the integrity of Avery's claims by insisting on seeing his records, a thing to which Avery refused to accede to because he felt that Herbert would 'nit-pick', and that his claims about reaching the Pole in the time he claimed, on a trip sponsored in part by the Prince's Trust, would be besmirched in controversy.

Over the years it is Peary's approach to navigation that has come in for the most criticism. Herbert produced a detailed hypothesis of how far off course the winds and currents might have carried him and he accused Peary of navigating like 'a rank amateur' making errors that "can only be described as astonishing"

Frederick Cook now has few proponents apart from his granddaughter and a small Society named after him -- and of course Rosemary.

Chapter 22
Arriving At The North Pole

One evening as we were lining up in another attempt to beat the Chinese to the buffet dinner, Laurie's soft Scottish voice came across the PA system.

"We expect to be at the exact North Pole just before midnight. All meet on the bow deck well wrapped up because there's a bit of a wind and the temperature is just under freezing so there will be a chill factor."

My thoughts went to past explorers who might have got to this point, or more likely had given up before they got here due to impossible conditions. First of all, we at least knew exactly where we were thanks to the ship's GPS the readings from which were screened throughout the ship showing us our exact position, drift or no drift. I thought of Peary and Matthew Henson certainly getting closer to the Pole than anyone before them (including Cook) and how at this point, only a score or so of miles away, they would be doing without stops for food or rest. They weren't like mountaineers who could see their goal right above them; they were in a flat wilderness, possibly in fog, now far away from the leads of water that might swallow them and on thick ice. Because of our GPS we knew precisely when we would arrive but Peary and the others would have had to make readings from the sun and horizon which was certainly not easy and at times, even impossible.

But we were going to be taken there, our stomachs full of good food and wine and the party that was planned for us when we reached the Pole was something old (and new) Polar explorers must have dreamt of.

As I was having my post-supper pre-arrival nap, Mohammed, sweating profusely, came back to the cabin. As usual he had been having an energetic game with a ball with the Russian crew and had missed both the announcement and dinner since he only ate once a day. I told him what had gone on and since we were not disembarking he had little interest in going back up on deck at midnight to watch people imbibe the 'evil alcohol'. I did however persuade him to join us and he agreed on condition that he did not have to wear the regulation bright yellow Parka with which we had all been issued; 'Ah' I thought,' a fashion-conscious Holy Man!'

On deck, just before midnight, we started to gather in the bow of the ship where the hotel crew and the two barmen were serving champagne (or a variant, I can never tell cheap from expensive) and the Chinese were photographing each other and anything else that moved. There was a party atmosphere; Burt and Roger had dressed in what they might have imagined sea monsters looked like and the rest of the crew were decked out in 'bottom of the sea' type costumes because they said that it was traditional to have an arriving-at-the-north-pole ceremony just like they do when you cross the equator in a ship! Phoney baloney, but since they were obviously trying, we went along with it. I had never heard the correlation between Neptune and the North Pole, but -- go figure!

Golf at the North Pole

Emotionally I found it very difficult to have arrived at the North Pole. I didn't have any surrealistic feelings, or any spiritual sensations -- I just thought It had come all too easy. I'd read about the intrepid explorers trying to get there before technology made it easy and there I was looking over the bow rail with a glass of champagne in my hand while thinking that other guys had resorted to cannibalism in order to get away from here.

I had spent the journey either sitting in a bar, eating great food in the dining area or lying in a comfortable bunk (thanks to Mohammed!) while those early explorers had had to make a decision as to whether to break through huge ice pressure ridges that might be the size of a two storey building or go to go around them, a task which might require a detour of several miles. As well as that, they, unlike us, did not have nuclear power, and so were drifting -- usually in an inconvenient direction.

One doesn't wish to exaggerate, but from the comfort of the ship, you could imagine being able to go to the North Pole nowadays with a snowmobile and a zodiac (polar bears permitting).

We were served with barbecued fish and meat and the excitement was whipped up by Laurie standing high in the bow à la Kate Winslett and Leonardo Di Caprio on that other ship. On the bridge a screen had been constructed so that we were able to watch the minutes between 89 and 90 degrees pass and finally we did a very slow count down (ships don't go very fast)--- Five, Four, Three, Two, One--- we were there, on the top of the world.

I looked for Mohammed but he had disappeared, so I carried on carousing with the other passengers knocking back barbecued fish and bits of meat washed down with 'fizzy'. Bob and Judy, his wife, were being photographed holding a beautifully made Stars and Stripes flag with 'Team USA' printed on it. I saw four Chinese gentlemen stripped to the waist holding an incomprehensible sign in Mandarin characters. Another group of fully clothed Chinese were running round the ship waving a large Chinese flag and the Californian Dennis and his wife (obviously elderly hippies) held out a sign for their photographs saying 'The United States of Consciousness'

The very rich American lady, Ginger, who had brought along her two teenagers was catching everything that was going on with a small video camera worn on a headband. The Australians, Evan and Grace, each had their own GPS and were busy photographing it to prove that they were definitely where Laurie told us we were.

Laurie did *faux* emotional in his little speech telling us to remember all the old explorers who had died in their attempts to get to where we were and then he stepped down from his perch to join us. After he had posed for the obligatory photographs with about 80% of the passengers I managed to get a word with him. He'd been taking these trips for a few years now and I asked him if a trip had ever failed to arrive.

Apparently, this had happened on one occasion due to the weather and there had almost been a mutiny among the passengers. The tour leader on that occasion had been female and because of threats, she did not leave her cabin again until they were back in Murmansk and all

Golf at the North Pole

the disgruntled passengers had disembarked. She either made her own way back from Murmansk or stayed on board because the anger among at least some of the passengers was intense. They had no 'come back' because in the small print of the very long contract each passenger had to sign, there is a get-out clause that covers 'failure to arrive'. It must have been very distressing because the cost of the journey was about twice the price of any other Arctic or Antarctic trip and the extra expense was obviously the attraction of being able to say that you'd been to the actual North Pole; no soft substitutes-- the <u>actual</u> North Pole.

But thankfully we'd arrived.

After an hour or so I went back to the cabin to find Mohammed already in bed. I asked him where he had disappeared to and he told me that his trip was now complete. Initially he had been a bit disappointed that although we'd stopped right over the North Pole they were not going to let us off because the ice was dangerously thin. We had been told to go back to bed and that during the rest of the night, the captain would sail around until he found an ice floe thick enough for us all to disembark.

That was the point when Mohammed decided to leave us. He had evidently got himself to the top deck and had done a bit of climbing to the highest point he could safely reach and there he'd prayed. He'd been nearer God when he prayed than anyone else had ever been (at least discounting aerospace travel).

At least one passenger had had a successful trip.

At breakfast the next morning I shared a table with a rather disappointed face-lifted American lady (not Rosemary). She had planned to do the 365 times walk round the Pole so that she could become a year younger but disappointedly she had to stay the same age. I did however tell her how marvellous her face lift was but I was rebuffed-- it was a lot of Botox!

I realised that our failure to disembark at the actual North Pole had caused a lot of disappointments, not least to my golf tournament that was now going to be a 'para'- North Pole Tournament.

I never quite found out where we actually stopped to do the 'North Pole things' that the Company had promised us. I know that it was still between 89 and 90 degrees -- but there's only one true 90 degrees North!.

After breakfast it was time for us to get off and sample the most northerly ice in the world.

On went the parkas, the gloves, the hats and the mufflers. All of that we expected, but we were also told we had to wear the rubber boots with which we had been provided, and since it would be possible to sink up to our thighs in slush the waterproof trousers had to hang over the tops of the boots to stop them filling.

At this point I was getting a bit disillusioned. I had spent a year reading every book I could get my hands on about the Arctic and I had girded my loins for wind, temperatures well below freezing, horizontal blizzard conditions and here I was, dressing as I might do to go out on a bad winter's day in Scotland when the snow was melting.

Golf at the North Pole

However I'd come to make a golf hole, a tournament and what I hoped might be history --- but we had to wait to disembark. First the Kalashnikov-carrying security guards went out onto the ice about half a mile from the ship to make sure there were no hungry polar bears waiting for their breakfast, but finding any would have been unusual because they seldom venture above 88 degrees north. They planted flags in the ice and slush, in a semicircle, to confine our movement within that area. The ship was our boundary on the other side and going past it was out of bounds and that might well have attracted more than a stroke and distance penalty.

At the bow, the anchor chain made a splendid prop for the photographers and so there was a constant procession of people taking photographs of their friends lying on, under, on top of and hanging from the chain.

At the stern the captain had kept one propeller turning to keep the sea from freezing and so there was about 25 metres of clear water for the hardy to do the 'Polar Plunge'. This had to be done with some care. The person stripped off to whatever layer they chose to keep on, had a security-belt fitted attached to a rope held by two of the crew and went down the steps into the water. Some jumped, some dived, some stepped in gingerly but the rather cuckoo Burt went in with a perfectly executed back somersault. I presumed that the belt was to help people out but I'm sure the planners back in America had made it compulsory so that if anyone suffered a cardiac arrest from the shock of the cold, the body could be recovered. I also spotted Ted, the fully qualified American Boarded Emergency Room doctor, squatting a decent distance away with his defibrillator so as not to alarm the plungers.

From the edge of the out-of-bounds came Mohammed, having fulfilled his ambition to pray once again on the ice at the top of the world. I was rather alarmed when he started to strip down to his underpants obviously intending to 'plunge'. He was pretty overweight and given the high incidence of heart disease among Saudis I thought him unwise but he seemed very calm (perhaps that's what prayer does for you) and probably since he had made his peace with God, he dived in and did a superb front crawl out into the sea for about 15 metres and then a classy back-stroke back. He of course declined the offer of vodka that all the others had devoured.

Those who had paid for another balloon flight waited eagerly for the opportunity to see even more ice and slush from the air but as far as I was concerned it was a nuisance because filling the balloon with hot air took up a lot of room on the ice floe making my golf course planning more difficult. The area alongside the boat was being set up with trestle tables and benches for a barbecue lunch and so I was eventually able to commandeer a 100-metre piece of ice away from everything and everyone else almost at the peripheral flags.

As I was doing all of this I had to accomplish one other promise. I had recently passed my audition to get into the Magic Circle and one of my friends was organising a Festival of Magic back in Edinburgh. He was an interesting man; originally a physicist he was working in a research lab when the chance came to enter a TV show called 'Fake It'. In order to prepare for this, Kevin had gone to London for three months, had taken lessons from Paul Daniels, Britain' premier magician, among others, and had managed to 'fool the experts' on the actual show.

He'd gone back to the lab -- for two days -- and then he'd resigned and decided to be a professional magician. I had taken a bundle of programmes with me and had them photographed against a sign saying 'North Pole'. It wasn't exactly at the North Pole but that's magic for you -- nothing is ever quite what it seems.

Chapter 23
Setting Up The Tournament

I wanted to create, at least as far as I could, a proper game of golf. Since we were only going to be at the Pole for a day I realised that to create 18 holes would be impossible even though we had 24 hours daylight. So I set about arranging a one-hole tournament in which all competitors would use the same balls and clubs.

I had brought with me several Srixon orange balls (no sponsorship, but one never knows what might flow from giving them a mention), a Cobra five iron, a cheap 58 degree wedge and an Odyssey putter; the latter might seem to be a bit extravagant but when you're a rubbish golfer you always blame your putting for the high scores and so one collects dozens of putters; I had several different types of Odysseys --- only the best will do!

Although not an Arctic expert of the Peary/Cook variety I knew that sticking a tee in the ice might be too difficult and thus a five iron would be a reasonable driving club from the flat and it could also be used for chip and run shots depending on the conditions.

Although because of global warming and melting of the ice cap the landscape lacked the drama described in the Arctic literature of the nineteenth century, I was delighted that I'd made the decision to go this year, because golf in the next few years might be impossible here. Since it was going to be the first North Pole Golf

Golf at the North Pole

Tournament, and possibly the last, I felt it only right that it should be organised as well as possible and that it should replicate the conditions of a golf tournament on dry land as accurately as possible.

I had not had the courage to walk up the back stairs in the R&A and ask for approval from Peter Dawson, our Chief Executive, who sits in probably the finest office in the western hemisphere. The furniture is perhaps not up to Madison Avenue standards but on one side he looks out over the Old Course at St Andrews and on the other he looks at the wonderful amalgam of the North Sea meeting the Firth of Tay. He freely admits that he has the best job in the world and although he sometimes steps down from Valhalla to join the Friday evening boozers in the Big Room, one feels that one cannot push too hard for favours. I'm sure if I asked him now however, Peter would freely admit that had he been asked he would certainly have have been delighted to have given my tournament the official blessing of the R&A; but to save him embarrassment I never asked.

Alan Feltham, the secretary of my Edinburgh club, The Bruntsfield Links Golfing Society was hugely enthusiastic and gave me his full support, but I asked him for neither sponsorship nor official recognition as a Club tournament. This was because Alan was new to his job and I did not feel it fair to create any further problems for him since he was at that time trying to deal with a course whose rising water table was threatening its very existence. He did however give me one of the flags that had been used in their 250th anniversary celebrations. It doesn't seem much to readers but if Bruntsfield is the course on which you've done your lowest round ever, there is a romantic attachment to the symbol of those 250 years of history.

Would I limit the tournament to non-Chinese only? Given the political correctness of the world in which we live, and even though no one of my age understands it, I knew I had a problem. But I did not identify any likely golfers among their numbers; their three main interests seemed to be taking pictures with huge lenses, eating all the food before anyone else could get there and playing Texas Hold'em. That I realised was 'selective racism' and as a professed 'liberal' I had to resolve this dilemma. Could I excuse their exclusion on the grounds of failure of communication? Neither I nor anyone else could speak Mandarin and none of the Chinese had approached any of us in conversation. Should I go round 50 people and say 'can you speak English?' That in itself might be construed as racist. So I made an executive decision -- this tournament would not be open to Chinese.

That limited the possible field to 48 geriatrics, Mohammed and myself. I knew that Mohammed had recently communed with God but I doubt that the subject of golf had come up in their discussions.

I realised that I was perhaps the only person among the passengers who was a regular golfer, but I wanted to create a field with people who had perhaps played the golf in the past, who might still play the occasional game, who had some knowledge of the Rules or who had the personal qualities required of a gentleman golfer-- I mean to say just because one is in the wilderness one's standards do not need to drop.

Golf at the North Pole

I had four groups of people to consider, but I could rule out three before I started. The Russian crew would almost certainly not be golfers. I've noticed over the years that life on the ocean wave and golf do not mix terribly well and even though golf in Russia is developing well, I don't think the game has become open enough for sailors.

The first course in Moscow was 'Virtual'. On 15 Sept 1987, an unlikely bunch of famous athletes swung symbolic golf clubs at imaginary balls when they launched the concept of building the first Moscow golf course. Among them were Mike Tyson (boxer), Pele (soccer player), and Sven Tumba (ice hockey).

However the course was finished two years later and in 1992 the Russian Golf Federation was created. In 1994 the second course, the Moscow Country Club, was opened but given the age and demeanour of the ship's crew I thought it would be a waste of time approaching them. Also I can't speak Russian

Then there was the hotel crew; largely Austrian with a few Russians. I ruled them out because they would all be working round the clock catering for our needs on the big day at 'the Big Nail'. I also have a grave suspicion of Austrians who play golf ever since a friend was refereeing a qualifying round for the British Open. He was following a game involving two top English amateurs whose fathers were acting as caddies and an Austrian who carried his own clubs and was obviously quite incompetent. As the round progressed it became slower and slower as they fell behind the groups in front and were holding up those behind. This was because the

Austrian did not seem able to hit the ball in a straight line and many of his shots that ended in the undergrowth had to be searched for. The two English golfers and their fathers complained to the referee accompanying the game-- and he was old enough to remember Maurice Flitcroft.

Now, if there was anything liable to upset my late friend Keith McKenzie, Secretary of the R&A, it was either the threat of anyone other than a 'great golfer' (Nicklaus, Palmer, Ballesteros, Watson etc) winning the Open or it was to hear the name 'Maurice Flitcroft'. Maurice was a former comedy stunt high diver, who worked as a crane-man in the shipyards of Barrow-in-Furness. He wanted to play golf and so bought himself a set of mail order golf clubs and read a book by Peter Alliss on 'How to Play Golf' which he had borrowed from the library. He could not afford the fees to join local golf clubs and so he used to hit balls on the beach, public parks and local playing fields.

In 1976 he entered the Open Golf Championship as a professional, not an amateur. He did this because, as an amateur, you have to produce a club handicap certificate but as a professional however, even if unaffiliated to club, you don't have to do so. He was therefore accepted as a *bona fide* entrant and got to play in a qualifying round, where he shot a 49 over par, 121.

This got him enormous publicity and for many years afterwards he kept trying to repeat the jape, playing a cat and mouse game with the R&A who always managed to spot who he was even though he used numerous aliases. To Keith, the Open Championship was the most

Golf at the North Pole

important thing in his world (apart from his wife Barbra) and he never saw the funny side of Flitcroft.

When the Austrian golfer mentioned above was causing a bit of a problem in the 2010 Open qualifying round the referee realised that if he turfed the Austrian off the course he'd end up designated as a 'blazer' in whichever newspaper had sponsored the situation. Very cautiously he radioed into the clubhouse to pass on his suspicions that he probably had a 'Flitcroft'.

The controller said, 'Hold on, and I'll get in contact with the Austrian Golf Federation'. A few moments later the response came. 'The Austrian Golf Federation confirm that the chap is indeed a registered professional golfer -- but he's hopeless!'

Then, back on board, we had the expedition crew. There were certainly some likely lads there but they would never be allowed time off to indulge in golf because their primary role for the day at the North Pole would be to make sure that the 100 people who got off the boat all got back on having done the compulsory thing of 'enjoying themselves'

So I had to pick my 'field' from the original limited group of passengers. In the end I found five bona fide players including myself, all of whom were motivated to get the title of North Pole Open Golf Champion of 2012.

Don and Shirley were of course included from an early stage and had remained enthusiastic even though Shirley still did not feel able to use right-handed clubs. She sportingly agreed to take part however with a three stroke handicap. Finally I persuaded Trevor, the New

A G D Maran

Zealand farmer who did not admit to playing regular golf to make up the numbers-- once an athlete, always....? And Dennis, having recovered from his Mig 29 experience was game for anything and admitted to having at one time been a good golfer.

So I had my competitors but I wanted to run a proper golf competition and with 50 photo crazy Chinese on the ice (minus the poker school) I had to keep the course clear.

That meant appointing Marshals. This is one golfing task at which I'm an expert and I can't remember how many golf tournaments at which I've marshaled. This is because marshaling is the sort of job the minor orders in a golf club must volunteer for to show that their hearts are in the right place even if the plane of their swing is somewhere else. Walker Cups, Open Championships, Dunhill championships, Club championships -- you name it, I've exerted my Hitlerian tendencies on any golfer or spectator who threatened to disrupt the smooth progress of whatever tournament it was.

Marshals have to be people whose presence commands respect and who have the personality required by someone in power to give a command in such a way that there is no alternative other than to obey. The call 'Back on the right please' must have sufficient command the first time to avoid it having to be repeated thus making the speaker sound angry.

For this task I chose my Italian friends. I did so on the basis of two considerations. Firstly, given the conditions we were about to face, ball spotting was going to be an important tasks for marshals situated on either side of the fairway, and since I had noticed that neither wore glasses either to read or to view polar bears or seals, they were ideal for election to this onerous position. The second consideration was that they were enthusiastic to help and given a title and a badge Italians will do anything. Both Gian Carlo and Maurizio, having been CEO's of major Italian industries, understood their roles with little instruction and I may say, with the distance of time, what a privilege it was to have such commanding men as my officials.

Ivor Robson has been the starter at the Open Championship since 1975 and has brought a *gravitas* to the simple matter of announcing players that has become part of championship golf folklore. With that beautifully soft Scottish accent he has announced all the "greats' for the past 40 years -- Palmer, Ballesteros, Nicklaus, Trevino, Player, Woods and countless others. I had heard him so many times that I was word perfect and was able to tutor Evan, the retired Australian financier, to repeat what Ivor might say had he been on the trip.

Evan came from Adelaide, and even though we had mutual acquaintances from that part of the world, he had managed to live his life out in that delightful town without ever playing Royal Adelaide. But he understood what was required.

"On the tee from America -- pause --- Bob (here the voice rises) Hamilton" (the voice falls as the '-ton' bit of Hamilton is reached.

The prospect of an Open Golf championship without Ivor is almost unthinkable and while I realised that there will probably never be another North Pole Open, I felt that standards should be as high as possible and so we had an announcer --but unfortunately no microphone ---but Evan did his best.

Two things remained to be sorted out, local rules and sponsorship.

Local rules can never override any of the 28 Rules of Golf but they allow of an interpretation of those Rules taking account of the local conditions. Before writing these, I had to be certain of the terrain over which we would be playing and so that was a task that would have to be postponed until I viewed the conditions on the patch of ice I'd selected.

Most people on the trip were fairly well off and none of the participants needed the prize money that I was going to raise but I thought that since all other tournaments have cash prizes this should be no different.

I had met the first 'possible' while waiting for my sightseeing helicopter flight over the ice fields. 'Call me Ginger' who had the fleet of Italian cars was an obvious target as was Bob.

the man who had turned up at the first cocktail party with immaculate black tie on a black edged smart evening shirt, while his wife also was dressed in very expensive clothes. In his lapel he had a badge with Olympic Rings. I had asked him what it represented and he told me that if you gave sufficient money to the US Olympic Committee, you got one!

Since I've always been 'rubbish' at asking women for anything, I found it easier to suggest to Bob that his name might be attached to the tournament if he put up

Golf at the North Pole

the prize money which would be symbolic rather than rewarding. I suggested $6 for the winner, $4 for second and $2 for third. As I say it was symbolic. I explained that I had no lapel badge to give him but listing himself as a sponsor of the North Pole Open while not perhaps enhancing his already large fortune might catch the eye should he declare it publicly.

In all seriousness Bob had probably never before been asked for a sum like this minus the usual three or four nothings at the end, but I assured him that it would all add to the success of what might turn out to be a 'world first'.

Chapter 24
The Tournament

My carefully thought out plans for clearing thick snow from an ice surface to create a fairway, leaving it piled at the sides for rough and completely clearing an area of snow to represent a green were wrecked when I saw the surface. We were on slush; difficult to clear and an impossible surface on which to make a green.

The speed that a golf ball travels over a green is measured as the stimpmeter reading which is a rather crude measure but adequate for the purpose. The greenkeeper uses a special piece of grooved metal that delivers a ball at exactly 6 feet/second on a flat piece of green, and after three runs in each direction he measures how far it runs (in feet) and that becomes the 'reading'. Most club greens are 9-10, many championships greens are as much as 12-13 but what I had in mind for my 'ice green' was 14-15, and to that end I'd been practising putting on linoleum for a month before the trip. As it was, slush did not allow a ball to roll any distance and we were going to have to play at stimpmeter 1-2.

It was not only disappointing but almost heartbreaking to have slush as the surface along with loads of, what in any other environment would be called, 'puddles' but which in golfing terms would be called 'water hazards'. I was going to have to run a tournament

Golf at the North Pole

that was basically entirely within a water hazard. If water is lying on a fairway on a normal golf course the player is allowed to move the position of the ball so that his feet are positioned on dry land. To do this in June in the Arctic would have required a return journey to Franz Josef Land.

But I'd come a long way for this and so something had to be created and we had to adapt to the conditions. Laying out a small tee ground was easy because all we needed was a small area on which to make a little hillock of snow on which to place the ball since it was impossible to insert a tee in the underlying ice for the tee shot. I found a seat for Evan to do his 'Ivor Robson' bit and that at least represented a start. Since he would have to sit still for some time, I sent someone to fetch him a Hot Toddy even though our watches said it was only early morning - - but at 90 degrees north there is no 'time'.

We all set to and cleared away as much of the slush as possible to identify a 70-80 metre length at the end of which we did a little more enthusiastic clearing but failed to come up with the beautifully clear ice surface I had envisaged for a fast green. Since we couldn't penetrate the underlying ice to make a 1.82-inch hole I took the flag of the Bruntsfield golf club (est. 1761) which Bill from Logistics had kindly mounted on a cane, and fixed it by piling a small cone of snow around it getting it as near two inches as I could.

Having set up the hole I then had to publish the carefully written local rules that I had already prepared. After a quick dash back to my cabin and the office printer, I was able to distribute a copy of the amended

A G D Maran

Local Rules to each of the other four competitors. They read as follows

THE NORTH POLE OPEN GOLF CHAMPIONSHIP 2012

This tournament will take place at (or near enough at) the North Pole on Sunday 1st July 2012. It will take place over 1 hole and the winner shall be the person who holes the ball in the fewest number of strokes.

Ladies will be allowed a handicap of one shot if right handed and three shots if left handed.

In the event of a tie there will be a play off from 20 metres and the player whose ball lies closest to the flag after one shot shall be declared the winner.

The game will be played according to the Rules of Golf as agreed by the Royal and Ancient Golf club of St Andrews and the United States Golf Association except where local rules deem otherwise.

LOCAL RULES

1 *If a ball is plugged through the green then it may be lifted cleaned and placed within one club length no nearer the hole*

2 *If the ball is plugged in any other place then it should either be played as it lies or declared unplayable when the player should proceed under Rule 28 ii (c)*

3 *The ball will be deemed to have been 'holed out' if it hits either the cone of snow around the base of the flag or the flagstick.*

4 *Should a ball be deemed unplayable behind a small iceberg then that iceberg should be considered as a moveable*

Golf at the North Pole

obstruction and the player may retreat under no penalty to another position keeping the small iceberg between himself and the hole.

5   All free standing water shall be deemed to be a lateral hazard and the player may proceed according to Rule 26

6   Any spectator interfering with the ball shall be treated as an outside agency and if caught should be placed in a puddle no nearer the hole.

We drew slips of paper for the starting order and when Gian Carlo and Maurizio were stationed on each side of the fairway, Evan announced the first player.

I was glad that I had come out first in the draw for starting times because I felt that by showing the others how golf should be played I would be able to set a shining example. The only drawback to this was that even when well-shod and dressed I was still a rubbish golfer

For the last 20 years I have never settled over a golf shot without worrying about a shank. To non-golfers I should explain that this is the golfing equivalent of cancer. Many years ago I had been a moderate golfer; not the sort of chap who wins anything, but able to play to a mid-range handicap. Then, out of the blue, I got cancer (a shank). What happens when you shank a ball is that instead of the ball leaving the club in a straight (or straightish) line it flies off sideways; in cricketing terms for those non-golfers, past cover point's left hand; and for those of you who don't even understand cricket, that means it goes at forty-five degrees to the intended direction of travel.

The great late Keith McKenzie once told me that when he had been invited to attend the opening of the new USPGA headquarters in Florida he heard a lecture by a famous teaching professional on the 17 different ways to shank. I know them all. Once you have suffered from 'the shanks' you are forever more afraid to hit the ball hard in case it flies off at even more of an angle; in fact one might worry that it could even, in the most severe cases, go backwards, but I've yet to do that.

But to get back to being afraid to hit the ball; it means that one's hand action is unconsciously delayed with the result that the ball is hit with the face of the club pointing sideways. I can accomplish this in any form of golf attire but if I am swaddled in waterproofs and cannot take the club back far enough to be able to rotate the shoulders, I shank. Thus, dressed in a padded yellow parka (although I have yet to experiment to see if colour affects my shank), a wooly hat and gloves, shoulder rotation is very limited and rubber boots settling into slush limit the footwork.

So, as my first shot sailed straight, if only for about 50 yards, I was pleased and relieved. My ball was lying in what I deemed was the fairway (roughly in the middle) and I then tried a chip and run, eschewing the lob wedge. Even though the chip and run is probably the most frequent shot played at St Andrews due to the nature of the ground, you should really first have a 'feel' for the ground conditions. Never having played at the North Pole before I was lacking in this skill and the ball went forwards a pathetic 10 metres. But now I was near the pin and so I did the same shot again with the same club and got to within a metre of the cone of snow holding the

Golf at the North Pole

flag. I knew putters had to be used if you are on the green on a normal golf course but here we were at the top of a world that is melting and the ball doesn't roll; so I hit it again with the mashie, and managed to bury the ball in the cone for a four.

Having decided that I was in charge of the rules and the organisation of this game, I took it upon myself, especially as I was now favourite to win or at least tie, to act as the marker which let me count the shots played by all the other competitors-- not that for a minute did I think that they would miscount, but Americans had invented the word 'mis-speak' and so there was no reason why they shouldn't also come up with a 'mis-count'

Evan's thinly-voiced Australian accent carried across the ice (a poor imitation of the great Ivor but...). *"On the tee, from South Carolina, America, Don Whiteman"*.

Now Don was the golf course 'collector' in the group and as he was also younger and more flexible than myself he was the opponent whom I considered to be the greatest threat. And I wasn't wrong. His first shot went just to the right of the green but it lay in slush. He had got the distance and from less than 10 metres he was, as they say, 'lookin' good'. But as every golfer knows it's the short game that wins tournaments and Don didn't cater for the unusual conditions, and decided to use the lob wedge. The lob wedge from snowy slush is not the club of choice. The ball went nowhere and Don got very wet. That possibly affected his mood, demeanour and concentration, because instead of reverting to the less lofted 5-iron he tried again -- quickly. Every time you hit a golf shot quickly, usually because you are annoyed at your previous effort, it is never a good shot. This was the case here and the result was the same as before -- no distance, lots of slush in the air, and even more on the parka. So from a very promising position he had 'blown it' and had one more shot to tie. At this point he was able to take time collecting his thoughts because he had had to wipe the slush from his face and eyes. His final shot with the 5 iron was brave but slightly sideways and he ended with a five. 'Oh what bad luck' I crowed . 'I thought you had it in the bag'.

He never replied.

We had a little pause before Shirley could get started. As I explained she was not only left handed but if she left her brain for medical research she might be the originator of a new syndrome. Obviously her absolute and total left-handedness was genetic in origin because had it been the result of an infection or a vascular accident she could not have survived since the brain damage would have been fatal. We tried everything.-- hitting with the back of the club, left hand below right, left hand only, using the short putter as a driving iron, etc. She was surrounded by people with formidable intellects. Both Gian Carlo and Maurizio had been top engineers, Evan had been a financial wizard, Don had been a pilot and though Dennis didn't seem to have much intellect he, at least, didn't try to confuse the situation. I said that we could not 'ignore' air shots but since she had a 3 shot handicap that would allow of the occasional miss. I feel that I should make a mental note to ask Mohammed how he would handle a situation like this in Islam.

Golf at the North Pole

Shirley did not do well. She had used her entire handicap by the time the ball had moved forwards five yards. She decided to post a No Return.

As Evan was about to announce Dennis I realised that he had disappeared. Now, missing a tee time is a serious business that can result in disqualification. Like everyone in St Andrews, the mother of the local butcher was a very good golfer, and one year had gained entry to the British Lady's Amateur Championship when it was being held in St Andrews. The family were not ordinary butchers. They had a farm, grew their own meat, owned the slaughter house and produced such good fare that people came from miles around to buy meat from her son who himself was a superb golfer.

This formidable lady was the sort of chief executive that today is very unfashionable and unpopular. She was guilty of micro-management. In other words she oversaw absolutely everything. Her tee time was 1.10pm and she arrived at 1.18pm to find herself disqualified. Since the shop was no more than 300 yards from the first tee, even the locals were surprised by her 'no show'. Her excuse was that she was reconciling the till!

Only in St Andrews!

Dennis's absence puzzled us. Since it was such a small field we did not want to lose a competitor especially since Shirley had already fallen by the wayside. We could always recognise Dennis from a distance because of his Hawaiian shirt and Bermuda shorts but even he had eschewed his normal dress to appear on the ice near the North Pole. We eventually found him trying to persuade some of the Chinese to enter. I was not at all pleased about that because I did not want the tournament to be another 'Britain's got Talent' competition and if Dennis was going around upsetting my arrangements I was not having it! With my limited vocabulary I was only able to intimate 'Later, later' but at least we now had a gallery. Dennis obviously enjoyed a gallery and was busy playing to it when I prompted Evan to do the 'on the tee from America' bit.

A couple of practice swings from Dennis let me know I was in trouble with my slender lead. He had obviously played a lot of golf and his swing was in the correct plane and even with lots of clothes on he was able to keep the central pivot still as he swung. He hit a fantastic shot, probably more than 150 yards.

However that was way beyond the Bruntsfield flag and way beyond Gian Carlo and Maurizio. Even if it hadn't been beyond them, both had reacted like soldiers under fire in a war and while stopping short of throwing themselves flat on the slush they had no idea where the ball had gone because of their evasive actions.

Dennis's new Chinese friends eagerly ran forward to find it -- but they didn't; and so he was left playing three off the tee. He did it again, and even though by now the area beyond the green was full of Chinese computer shop owners, they couldn't find the ball either as it was plugged in deep snow. I only had three balls left and so I suggested to Dennis that five off the tee would accomplish nothing apart from leaving Trevor bereft of a chance to win. He decently retired from the competition and resumed his dealings with the Chinese. Perhaps he

Golf at the North Pole

was an arms dealer or the sort of person that needs to make business contacts; but I never asked him.

Evan again. *"On the tee, Trevor Hardcastle from New Zealand"* I felt he said it with perhaps too much Antipodean favouritism. I whispered to him that Ivor never ever showed favouritism for Scottish players even though often encouraged by the crowds. But if you live in Adelaide, what can you know! Then Trevor, the sort of New Zealander who picked up British rugby players and threw them around before eating them, did much the same as Dennis. Admittedly he had two air shots before he made contact but he hit a phenomenal shot further than any previous one. It went straight for about a quarter of a mile before turning sharp left and passing between the faces of two Chinese, not having been persuaded by Dennis to join us, who were having a conversation. We were very fortunate the ball stayed in space and not in a Chinese cheek-bone.

I ran forwards to apologise but was met with the sort of implacable anger that the British and American troops must have faced when they went to war in Korea 50-odd years ago. 'Who did this, who did this?" they screamed. My Chinese did not extend to telling them that New Zealand farmers were a sort of different breed who seldom understood anything beyond the touchlines and the in-goal areas. Trevor did apologise but it was not accepted. So he said, using New Zealander adjectives that would not be understood in Beijing but would be normal syntax in Glasgow, "What else can I do apart from apologise?" Well these were not exactly the words he used but it's enough to give you the drift.

By now lots of other Chinese had gathered and I wondered if they were computer shop keepers or Triads who had been rewarded for having achieved their murder quota for the year.

I suggested that since the official tournament had finished they could have the remaining golf balls and clubs and also any others that they could find 'out there', and that seemed to get a general acceptance. It took about 10 minutes for them to lose the remaining balls by which time I managed to retrieve the Bruntsfield flag (the secretary wanted it back; he's a bit of a prude).

I looked for Mohammed hoping to get some words of peace and forgiveness that might settle the situation but he had gone off to play volley-ball with the Russian crew.

Chapter 25
Coming Home

We arrived back in Murmansk where once again we were driven to the airport in the July rain, each one of us praying that there will not be another tour (by this time Mohammed has been anointed as the Holy One, delegated by those who did not have a God to pray for them).

He must have done a good job because instead of driving round for another tour of a nether world we drove directly to the airport passing miles of tundra and reindeer farms with never a soul in sight.

In spite of gloomy Greg's warnings about the dreadful fate that awaited us from the Russian custom officials if we had not filled in our forms correctly, we never saw any sign of them and the lack of security at the airport reminded me of the olden pre-terrorist days when one arrived at an airport, handed in one's luggage and got on a plane. But there would be absolutely no reason to blow up Murmansk unless done as an act of kindness to the local inhabitants.

It was a Saturday (that also came as a surprise since I hadn't considered naming days for two weeks) and Helsinki was deserted since that was the norm in the summer. Most Finns have a place in the country to which they emigrate every Friday evening, the Finnish capital taking on the aspect of a ghost town. Once, when visiting a friend in Finland, he had told me that when he constructed his first country house beside a lake (in Finland all country houses are beside lakes) the first structure he built was the sauna house on the side of the lake. This would be but a short walk from the house and the lake would be used for the cool part of the 'sauna ceremony'.

This time I shared a room with a man from Oklahoma who I could swear I had never seen on the cruise. I probed to see if he had actually been on the journey and we talked about the rather mundane medical subject of sore backs while we each dealt with a two week supply of emails.

Of course as a retiree I'm always astonished at the grief that e-mails causes my younger friends when they talk about the bore of wading through hundreds a day, but trawling through more unread emails than I'd ever seen before in my life I found it a rather pleasant way of spending an hour -- of course, all the time dutifully replying as best one can as a head and neck surgeon to questions from my room mate about lower back pain.

The first thing I did on returning to St Andrews was to go to the R&A to seek out the 'oldest member'. This is a hallowed position in the club. The holder of the post will have been a member for at least 50 years, he will have a locker in the Big Room, he will no longer play golf and will be referred to whenever there is a dispute about club history. He will know every member even though it has been years since he has set eyes on them and he will also be able to provide a reasonable family tree for those who are interested. He will occupy the

Golf at the North Pole

armchair by the bay window so that he has the finest view of the first tee and fairway and the first thing any member, new or old, should do on entering the Big Room is to offer to buy the oldest member a drink. The oldest member, by dint of age, usually has a life span of only four or five years but in those years he is a very important personage.

Mere members occupy the ground floor of the Club and above us reside the officials who run the game of golf throughout the world. The upper floors are referred to as Camp David and those who reside there have names one dare not mention, in the same way as Harry Potter declines to talk about Voldemort. If one wants soundings about opinions held by those who rule us we ask the oldest member who could probably be considered the earthly representative of those above us in Camp David.

The present oldest member is a retired ex-Army officer, perpetually grumpy since his Regiment was axed, presenting a fair but unsmiling countenance.

After buying him a Club number 2 whisky I said ' Arthur, I have this terrific idea for a book about the North Pole Open where I won a Golf Championship'.

'Arnie, you're the worst golfer in the Club and you've entered more 'No returns' than anyone else in the monthly medals. Was this some sort of Paralympics open only to the lame, defective and paralysed'

'Arthur, be serious for a moment, I've been to the North Pole, arranged a golf tournament and with a par four, I won it'

'So' said Arthur.

'Do you think if I went upstairs and asked Peter or Aubyn if I could write about not only this but also tales from the Big Room, what would they say?'

'Probably 'Get lost and don't ever bring the subject up again''

'You don't really mean that. I mean very few members have been to the North Pole and even fewer have won a championship there'. I continued more in the hope than the belief that the advice would change.

'Arthur, be reasonable. I'm a member of the greatest golf club in the world and I've played golf successfully on top of the world-- does that not give me a passport to Camp David?'

'No' said Arthur.

'So if I write about the Club, the foibles of some members and tales from the Big Room, even as some sort of champion, you think I'd be in trouble?'

'With a capital 'T' ' he replied.

'So I can't write about the history of the Club and its role in Golf?

'No'

'And I can't write about stories I've heard over the years in the Big Room -- or colourful members'

'You could, but you'd get the boot'.

His boredom with the conversation was shown when he did a thing the oldest member never does-- he rang the bell and ordered himself another club number 2. It was at this point that my mind flashed back to a

Golf at the North Pole

conversation in cabin 85 when Mohammed instructed me on the evil effects of alcohol.

I gave up St Andrews and went to my golf club in Edinburgh whose flag had graced the polar ice and which effort had been accompanied with the good wishes of the secretary, Alan Feltham.

Bruntsfield is a club for elderly golfers where members never talk about aptitude for the game. In fact on one occasion when I was pencilling-in the result of a club match and was about to put down the fact that I'd lost by 6 & 5, a past captain came behind me, put his hand on my shoulder and said 'In this club my boy we never lose by more than 2 & 1'.

I should have realised that this certainly would be the case in a club where the cut-off age for the Junior championship is 50.

The elderly cohort of regulars, most of whom have not acquired computer literacy nor wish to explore the internet seem to appreciate the fact that Alan, the Secretary, communicates with the young by email while always making sure that the information is imparted to the computer illiterate.

I went to his office and handed back the flag (minus the pole, which Bill (logistics) had taken back to Toronto. He was more relieved than I expected to get it back because there were only a few of the special ones created for the club's 250th anniversary left from the previous year. I did wonder about his fondness for it because once a flag has the figure 250 printed on it there is little point in using it a year or two later but the understanding of this mystery is why Alan is a golf club secretary and I'm a mere member.

However, after he had been reassured that everything he had given me to take away had been returned, he invited me to send him some photographs and also a description of the event.

He was extremely kind in distributing this to all the members in his weekly newsletter which let them see that even though I was in the tenth percentile of the worst golfers in the club I had finally achieved something albeit in a very small field . . . though in a remarkable location.

Alan got it all wrong. He put in the photograph of Don about to play his errant fourth shot. But he's a very busy man.

Will I be the last North Pole Open Golf Champion? Possibly, because the ice cap is melting.

There is a big difference between the effects of global warming in the Arctic and the Antarctic. The Antarctic is virtually unaffected by global warming, while the ice cap in the Arctic is shrinking as you read these words. Between 1987 and 2011 it has shrunk from 7.5 million square kilometers to 4.6 million, which is an area equivalent to the size of India.

NASA in the past has made many forecasts which have proved wrong, but they announced recently that the polar ocean will no longer be frozen in the summer after 2013. That is probably pessimistic but by 2020 the top of the planet will certainly be free of ice in the summer.

In 2008 for example a satellite found that for the first time in over 100,000 years both the north-west and the north-east passages were open at the same time. The truth of this was confirmed when Sarah Palin who said that that would be impossible! But in the same year tourists had to be evacuated from Baffin Island's Auyuittuq National Park because of flooding from thawing glaciers.

Monitoring sea ice is a fairly recent activity. It began seriously in the 1950s using instruments available on nuclear submarines. Satellite monitoring started in 1979, and since then the Arctic ice has shrunk by 12% per decade. Using evidence from Viking sagas, whaling records, pollen records, log books, the debris shed by melted ice rafts, diatoms (algae), ice cores and tree rings, scientists have constructed a record of the Arctic past which suggests that the summer sea ice is at its lowest level for at least 2000 years. Six of the hottest years have occurred since 2004 and according to the Intergovernmental Panel on Climate Change (IPCC) the last time the polar regions were significantly warmer was about 125,000 years ago.

This can be regarded as the 'death spiral' of the Arctic ice cap and it is certain that rather than using the north-west and north-east passages for waterways from the Atlantic to the Pacific, sailing directly over the North Pole will be an option, because as well as shrinking in area the ice is shrinking in thickness.

If the north polar ice cap melts it won't make a jot of difference to the levels of sea water in the world because the ice is already in the sea. The effect of ice melting to form water is similar to the effect of the melting ice cubes in your gin and tonic -- the level of fluid in the glass stays the same because the amount of displacement equals the amount of fluid added as the ice cube melts.

On the other hand if the thousands of metres of ice over the land of Antarctica melted, we'd either all drown or be living on the Alps, Himalayas or Rockies.

The effect of the Greenland glaciers melting is going to be somewhere between these two extremes and therefore will be of great significance. The Greenland icecap is moving into the Atlantic at an increasing speed. In the one hundred and fifty years between 1850 and 2000 it moved 40 Kilometers but in the 5 years between 2001 and 2006, it moved 20 kilometers.

The thickness of the sea ice has also decreased. Between 1958 and 1976 it averaged 3 metres which was a lot less than that reported by explorers at the beginning of the century; the thinning has however continued and the average between 1993 and 1997 was just over a metre.

There are two main reasons for this. One is the rise in the sea temperatures and the other is a prolonged eastward shift in the early 1990s in the Arctic winds known as the Arctic oscillation. This moved a lot of ice from the Beaufort gyre, a revolving current in the western Arctic, to the ocean's other main current, the Transpolar Drift Stream which runs down the side of Siberia. As a result of this, a lot of thick multi-year ice was flushed into the Atlantic and has not been replaced.

The world's temperature began to rise in 1961, and by 2010 it was higher than at any time since the dinosaurs became extinct. All of this has been well documented and while we all accept that global warming is happening, it is doubtful if we are going to do anything about it.

Firstly, it is going to be very expensive, and we are in a global recession with all spending reduced in every country, and secondly, since it would need everyone everywhere to do their bit, it is clearly not going to happen. Solutions keep being promulgated but the bottom line is -- money.

People will have to find a 'magic bullet' such as put forward by Professor David Keith of Harvard who suggested geo-engineering or, in catchy modern phraseology, 'planet hacking'. This would involve solar radiation management or reflecting sunlight back into space. Keith's idea is to transport enough sulphur into the stratosphere to create a haze with the same cooling effect as a volcanic eruption such as happened with the eruption of Mount Helena in Canada in 1980. Such processes are very controversial because of the possibility of dramatic and damaging side-effects.

Some of this is taking place already because of industrial pollution from countries bordering the Arctic. Since the 1950s, pilots have noticed a gradually increasing Arctic 'haze' which is made up of dry sulphate particles as well as soot and some soil from the heavily industrialised parts of Europe.

There are eight countries with some land-sea interface with the Arctic Ocean but for most of them global warming does not present a threat; in fact a doubling of temperature in chilly Greenland would be welcomed by the residents. However if the ice goes, then the region could warm up even quicker because of what is known as the Albedo effect which is when the dark water now exposed by the melted ice absorbs even more of the sun's heat; this will speed up the melting of the ice, since black absorbs more heat than white.

On the plus side the melting Arctic ice cap is an opportunity for resource development and the enlargement of shipping activities and the service industries that will surround these.

Arctic oil however will also make a big difference to global supplies and as long as the Arctic governments continue the harmonious co-operation that they have shown to date then they will all prosper.

But from the comfort of the large veranda window in the ship's bar all I could think of is ice or water-- and I'm astonished at the amount of water. Only a few weeks ago a new record was set for the amount of Arctic sea ice that melted in the summer, a level that even outpaced the predictions made by the United Nations' climate experts; over a 24 hour period, 97% of the ice was found to be in a melting state.

NASA's forecast of the Arctic Ocean reverting to water in the next few years seems to be not far off the mark. Before boarding the *50 years of Victory* I'd read many polar travellers' tales which were constant in one thing and that was the enormous difficulty they had of getting their supply sledges and themselves over the ice ridges that could be the size of a building. If the North polar explorers went too early, then the winter storms and the pressure ridges would be too tough, but if they were caught on the north polar ice cap in the summer then they would be floating on ice floes that may be separated by large lakes.

So I was glad to have gone at a time when the Arctic bore some resemblance to the tales that I had read of the old explorers and I could also see why some of them had been transfixed by the beauty of the wilderness of which I was now Golf Champion.

Had I been younger I would have planned to go back -- if it's still there.

A G D Maran

Acknowledgements

I suppose logic suggests that the tour company, Quark, should thank me for giving them an enormous amount of money to take me to the North Pole but on the other hand, had they not been in the 'take you to the Pole' business then I'd never have arrived at the top of the world and this book would not have been created. So, on balance, I think I should thank them for providing not only the boat, *50 years of Victory,* but a splendid expedition crew, excellent food and wine and captivating lectures.

I have changed the names of passengers and crew but those who want to recognise themselves will undoubtedly be succesful-- but they'd be wrong! They were all splendid company for the two weeks of the trip and have left me with many happy memories..

I have singled out Mohammed who shared my cabin. I have known dozens of people from all the Middle Eastern countries and because of that I was in sympathy with him from the start; there were no surprises and all my descriptions are based on admiration and fondness for a remarkable young man.

Perhaps my description of the Chinese passengers might be interpreted as cruel but it is far from that. We are just now in the position of not being able to understand the language of the worlds' fastest growing country; but whose fault is that? I am sure there are thousands of Chinese school children who are studying English with an Asiatic energy that would put to shame the weak efforts of some of my grandchildren to learn Mandarin. At my age of course I remain the arrogant, ignorant Britisher abroad.

I am grateful to my old friend, Dr John McKendrick, for reading and criticising the early drafts with the eagle eye he has demonstrated from the time we were fellow students in the fifties in Edinburgh University.

When I thought I had reached a final draft, Debs Warner, the person who edited my Mafia book, assured me that it was far from finished and needed at least another couple of drafts. I have grown to admire her judgement so much that my acceptance of her opinion is now unquestioning.

I am grateful to my friend Patricia Clough, late of Reuters, the Times and the Independent, for permission to publish an abbreviated version of the story in chapter 12 about the stranded German weather crew at the end of the War. If you want to read the full version of the story you will have to do it in German since it is in a book called Mein Germany which is, at the moment, only published in German.

A G D Maran

Also, while the story of Vincenzo Lombardi landing his balloon in St Andrews is well known I first read it in a wonderful book about the town by my fellow R&A member, Mike Tobert, *Pilgrims in the Rough.*

Finally, those men whose untiring work makes the lives of golfers so pleasant, The Members' Secretaries, Aubyn Stewart-Wilson of the R&A and Alan Feltham of the Bruntsfield Links Golfing Sociaty, Edinburgh. If I painted the wrong picture of you please try to forget it at the next meeting of the handicap committee.

Finally my thanks go to Anna, my wife of 50 years, who indulges my fear of dementia and accomodates my foible of believing that researching and writing are a prophylaxis against madness.

Bibliography

Amundsen R	My Life as an Explorer: Doubleday, New York 1928
Avery T	To the End of the Earth: Atlantic Books, London 2009
Barrow J	Voyages in the Arctic regions: Harper&Bros, New York 1846
Bryce R	Cook and Peary: The Polar Controversy Resolved Stackpole Books, Mechanicsburg, PA 1997
Burch E	The Eskimos: Norman and London; Univ of Oklahoma Press 1988
Carroll,L	The Walrus and the Carpenter: Through the Looking Glass, Penguin Popular Classics 2003
Clough P	Mein Germany -- Deutschland vo innen und aussen DTV; Munich 2013

Cook F	My Attainment of the Pole Polar publishing; Pittsburgh (reprint) 2001
Counter S A	North Pole Legacy; Black, White and Eskimo; Invisible Cities Press, 2001
Cross W	Disaster at the Pole; The Lyons Press, Guildford, 2002
Dither E	The Truth about Nobile; Williams and Norgate, London, 1933
Ellis Richard	On thin Ice; Alfred A Knopf, New York 2009
Fleming, F	Ninety Degrees North; The Quest for the North Pole; Grove Press New York, 2001
Fleming, F.	Barrow's Boys; Granta Books London 2001
Guttridge, L F	Ghosts of Cape Sabine; The Harrowing True story of the Greely Expedition; Berkley Books, New York. 2000
Henderson, B	Fatal North; Adventure and Survival Aboard USS Polaris; The First U.S. Expedition to the North Pole; New American Library, New York 2001
Henderson B	True North; WWNorton, New York, London 2005
Herbert W	The Noose of Laurels; Doubleday, New York, 1990
Huntford R	Nansen: The Explorer as Hero; Barnes and Noble Books 1998

Jackson, F	The Lure of Unknown Lands; G Bell and Sons 1935
Kane E	Arctic Explorations; Nelson, London 1892
Lachambre H	Andrees Balloon Expedition; Ulan Press 2012
Loomis C	Weird and Tragic Shores; The Story of Charles Francis Hall, Explorer; Modern Library, New York, 2000
Lundborg, E	The Arctic Rescue; Viking, New York, 1929
McGhee R	The Last Imaginary Place; Oxford University Press 2005
Moss, S	The Frozen Ship; The Histories and Tales of Polar Exploration; Blueridge New York, 2006
Nansen F	Furthest North; The Epic Adventure of a Visionary Explorer; Harper and Bros, New York, 1897
Nansen F	Adventure and other papers; Leonard and Virginia Woolf, London 1927
Nobile, U	With the Italia to the North Pole; Dodd Mead, New York, 1931
Peary R	Nearest the Pole; Doubleday Page & Co New York 1907
Poe, Edgar A	The Narrative of Arthur Gordon Pym; OUP, 2008

Rawlins D	Peary at the North Pole;Fact or Fiction; Robert B Luce, Washington 1973
Schama S	Landscape and Memory; Alfred A Knopf, New York 1995
Shandrick M	The Duke of Abruzzi ; Mountaineer's Books, London 1997
Shelley M.	The Modern Prometheus; Broadview Press, 1818
Sundman, P	The Flight of the Eagle; Pantheon, New York 1970
Tryde, E A	De döda på Vitön: sanningen om Andrée; Stockholm: Bonnier. (Swedish) 1952
Vaughan R	The Arctic:A History; Alan Sutton, Stroud 1994
Verne J	Journey to the Centre of the World; Pierre-Jules Hetzel, 1864
Weems, J	Peary: The Explorer and the Man; Houghton Mifflin Co, Boston 1967
Wilkinson A	The Ice Balloon Expedition; Fourth estate, London, 2013
Woodman, R	Arctic Convoys 1941-1945;Pen and Sword Maritime, London 1994
Wright, T	The Big Nail; The John Day Co, New York,1970

PERIODICALS

National Geographic Sept 1988

Hampton's Magazine January 1911

Congressional record; 61st congress; 3rd Session 1911 Vol53

New York Times Sept 7-9th 1909

New York Herald Sept 10 - 6 December 1909